Origamidō

First published in the United States of America by
Rockport Publishers, Inc.
33 Commercial Street
Gloucester, Massachusetts 01930-5089
Telephone: (978) 282-9590
Facsimile: (978) 283-2742

ISBN 1-56496-639-9

10 9 8 7 6 5 4 3 2 1

Design: Leeann Leftwich
Cover art, *Buddha Mask*, by Akira Yoshizawa.

Printed in China.

Origamidō

THE ART OF FOLDED PAPER   MICHAEL G. LAFOSSE

QUARRY BOOKS

THIS BOOK IS DEDICATED to the memory of Mrs. Emiko Kruckner, whose love of origami art energized her emissarial efforts to widen the appreciation of Yoshizawa sensei's monumental contributions. As liaison and friend, Emiko made possible for many a more richly rewarding life in Origamidō.

contents

INTRODUCTION
Origamidō: The Way of Paperfolding

Today, the Japanese word origami (ori, "fold," kami, "paper") is used to represent various kinds of paperfolding activities and its final product (do, "the way") is the experience or "path" taken to get there. Each person comes to origami with his or her own set of potentials and ambitions, coupled with their culture, special interests, and temperament. Creatively, they find their own way, each person adding that which only he or she could have found.

Paper

Paper, the all-essential medium of origami, is not one single substance but a rich family of materials. Paper is formed from plant fibers, the processing, blending, coloring, and forming of which lead to a seemingly infinite range of possibilities. A large part of the success of many origami designs comes from careful choice and preparation of the paper. Consider the simple paper dart, attributed to Leonardo da Vinci. One would not fold a successful paper dart from a paper towel—it would be too soft. A stiffly starched, crisp sheet would work better. The creases would then stay firmly in place and the form would possess the rigidity required for efficient gliding.

Initially, the writing system of the Orient employed brush and ink on silk, and paper was developed later as a reasonable replacement for the expensive silk. Such papers accommodated the Oriental writing tools by being soft and absorbent. Later, paper would face European writing tools and methods and so it had to be reformulated to mimic the hard-surfaced sheepskin parchment, which would withstand the quill pen. Perhaps it is not coincidence that the invention of the paper dart had to wait for Leonardo da Vinci and the crisply sized papers of Europe. Only then did it have the qualities necessary for making good airplanes, which has led to thousands of wonderful designs in this category of paperfolding.

The artwork, *George L. Mountainlion*, in the process of being created by the author, Michael LaFosse, at the Origamido Studio.

Cooked cotton rags being beaten into pulp.   Color is added.   A view of the mould and screen.   Pouring a sheet.

Relatively few folded-paper designs can be traced back, with any certainty, to antiquity. Perhaps more than 80 percent of the many thousands of models were actually designed within the last century, and the majority of those models only within the last fifty years. Most of the creators of these models are still alive today. It is for this reason that I find it amusing whenever I hear someone say "the ancient art of origami."

Designing a new origami model requires plenty of paper and ample free time: both are relatively modern commodities. Today, paper is everywhere and few people have any trouble putting their hands on some paper to fold. With all of this paper, and so many eager minds working through any challenge that origami may propose, it is no wonder that the art has arrived.

Invention and Style

One would think that everything that can be done with a square sheet of paper has already been done before. Where do you go to find out how to fold an elephant? The local library? It is often not obvious to many people that they have the power to create new, original origami. So, how does one create? How does one develop particularly clever folding patterns? Most people find a folding pattern in a book, in an origami kit, or on a videotape. Invention often begins by modifying these existing models to taste. Invention can also begin by forgetting how to fold something you once knew how to fold. Often folders fumble or fiddle with bases until they discover interesting shapes and possibilities. As one develops a fluency in the language of origami, the creating artist better understands the structure systems and their possibilities in folded paper. Expert folders use this understanding to plan more deliberately and design more surely and successfully. Each designer asserts his or her own taste and favorite topics.

Expert folders eventually develop a characteristic style that often becomes obvious to even casual observers, just as most of us can recognize styles in music, painting, writing, sculpture, or dance.

Techniques

There are no real rules in origami. Many think that origami must always be folded from single uncut squares of paper, but there is nothing to substantiate that. In fact, much of the earlier origami work of the Japanese regularly included scissor cuts and multiple-element constructions. Early practitioners of the art did not have such a highly developed arsenal of origami techniques as those that exist now—many of which have been developed to eliminate cutting.

Removal of frame (deckle).   Laying sheet onto vacuum table.   Vacuum table presses the sheet and removes much of the water.   Sheet on support felt, ready for drying.

Relatively short, easy-to-remember folding sequences promoted the techniques most successfully passed on until the advent of published books on origami, which greatly facilitated the preserving and sharing of new ideas worldwide. Gradually, origami has become rich with advanced folding techniques. Consequently, modern origami practitioners embraced the concept of working without any cutting, and since adopting this convention, designers have pushed themselves to tackle the big challenges. With so many of the technical issues out of the way, there has been a growing movement to improve upon the refinement of design and the artistic potential. Such improvements in the art pave the way for books like this.

Much of the origami art presented in this book is wet-folded, a technique pioneered and popularized by origami master Akira Yoshizawa. Yoshizawa made the soft papers of Japan more suitable for origami by stiffening them with starch paste, pasting two sheets back-to-back. This technique is often referred to as back-coating, a standard technique in the Orient used to stiffen paper to make it suitable for book covers and box making. This very stiff paper necessarily required a little softening before folding, so Yoshizawa lightly dampened the paper with water. While wet, the paper was pliant and responsive. Soft, rounded folds could be introduced into the design. When the paper dried, the starch hardened and the model would retain its shape indefinitely. Today, there are many devotees to this wet-folding method. The wet-folding approach can also be applied to stiff, heavy art papers, which would otherwise be unusable for most origami.

A dry method that approximates wet-folding is the tissue-foil method, where ordinary kitchen aluminum foil is bonded to some kind of thin paper. Sometimes the foil is papered on one side, sometimes both. The foil's malleable and compressible properties mimic the wet-folding effect. The downsides to this technique are that the foil stays soft and is easily misshapen, and the foil and most of the adhesives used in the bonding process deteriorate over time and so these works are not considered permanent.

Mastering an Origami Model

No matter how simple or complex any origami model may be, mastering it will require several stages of effort. First, and most obvious, you must learn the folding sequence. This is similar in many ways to learning a piece of music from the first note to the last. Along the way, you may encounter difficulty and you will focus on these trouble spots until you are accomplished at these new techniques. It is only after you have gotten this far that you can begin to realize the true potential of an origami design.

Many folders follow a checklist approach to tackling origami models, folding a model once or twice and then moving on to the next. There is some merit in this approach for the beginner, when one is intent on learning the many intricacies of origami technique and structure. But to be able to create truly inspiring work, it is best to select even just a few origami models, of subjects that most interest you, and make a long-term study of them. Over the years you may try these designs in many papers. Each paper will present you with new challenges in folding the form.

Even an origami model reveals what the folder does and does not understand about the subject. If your origami is of some kind of animal or plant, you should observe these living subjects firsthand; the next time you fold the origami you will see a significant improvement. Additional touches like these mark the distinction between origami craft and origami art, and are the source of satisfaction that make creators and accomplished folders continue to fold throughout their lives.

Many folders develop astonishing technical proficiency in their teens, creating with abandon and great enthusiasm. Revisiting their earlier models later in life, they many find that their aesthetic appreciation has changed and grown and clearly shows in the work. This opportunity to change with maturity is seen in other artists, from Picasso to Beethoven, and is often a hallmark of serious lifelong artists.

This book reveals the richness and depth of the world of modern origami by showcasing some of the most imaginative and delightful examples of the art available today. This is not a how-to book. You will not find diagrams for the folding of many of these models. Rather, it is an international exhibition of origami in book form.

At the end of this book, the sources for published folding instructions to all of the featured works are included, except for the few for which such information does not yet exist. I have also included a worldwide listing of origami organizations, artists, and Web sites: many origami enthusiasts work in isolation, not knowing anyone else who folds or where to find good books and papers. I hope this book will bring these people together as well as introduce the art to the uninitiated.

An inspiration to fold will likely result from viewing the exquisite pieces in this volume, so I have included the diagrams for a few projects at the back of this book. These models were chosen from each section to give you a taste of different styles and to further your understanding of the language and process of origami.

Selected shots of the folding of *George L. Mountainlion.*

ANIMAL, VEGETABLE, & MINERAL

PAPERFOLDERS USE THEIR ART TO TRANSLATE THE WORLD AROUND THEM, just as writers, painters, actors, and sculptors do. This section features masterful renditions inspired by the natural world. The origami models featured here range in complexity from a single fold to models of extraordinary detail. Several brilliant models are compound, or multipiece, constructions, such as the dinosaur skeletons or Kawasaki's Rock Crystal. These practical solutions to paperfolding challenges help dispel the myth that the best origami pieces are always brought forth from a single sheet of paper.

One thing that these paper artists all share is a passion for their chosen subjects. Many have spent countless hours of dedicated observation and study of the natural model for their subjects, fueled by an intense desire to bring it to life in paper.

These hummingbirds feeding on Jacobina blossoms show how different origami elements can be used effectively in a composite display. The paper, made by hand, was formed from iridescent purple pulp on one side (showing only on the chin of the male), while a deep, iridescent green-colored pulp was screened and pressed onto the purple pulp, forming a duo–colored paper. Jacobina blossoms are often in different stages of bloom—some budded, others already wilted—which the artist was careful to illustrate. Each bird, leaf, or blossom of this composition is folded from a single square of handmade paper and assembled on wire. The paper was made by Michael LaFosse from plant fibers of Sonora Desert origin.

Arizona Hummingbirds

Michael LaFosse
USA
Life–size

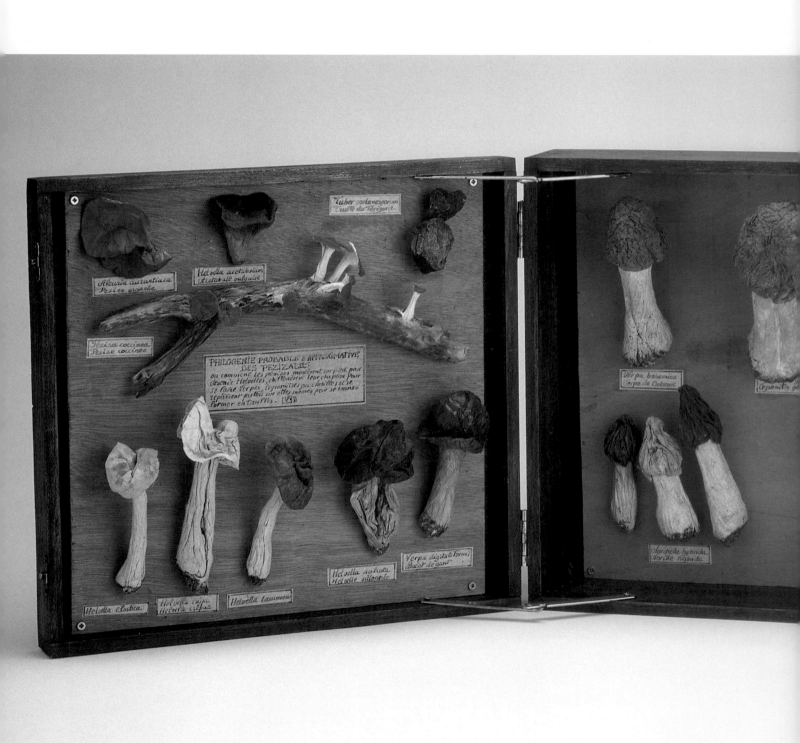

Mushrooms

Vincent Floderer
France
Life-size
Wet-folded from a variety of papers.

It was Floderer's intent on that the process of folding these mushrooms be expressive in a natural and organically developmental way that would imitate the growth and the unfolding of living mushrooms. Floderer was inspired by, and has adapted, Paul Jackson's paper-crumpling techniques to create scores of different species of mushrooms. The paper was well soaked in water at some point during the shaping, then molded and left to dry. Floderer used several types of paper, which he selected to match the colors and textures of the types of mushrooms portrayed; in some cases, he applied paint and other surface treatments.

Pangolin

Eric Joisel
France
Approximately 22" long (56 cm)
Folded from hand-tinted Kraft paper.

For many, the pangolin has been the holy grail of origami. Creating the numerous scaly plates that cover this distinctive animal's hide without producing a tortured and bulky form presents a formidable technical challenge, mastered here by Eric Joisel. The pangolin was so technically demanding that it took several days to complete.

Samurai Helmet Beetle,
Allomyrhina dichotomus

Daniel Robinson
USA
Paper made by Daniel Robinson in collaboration with
Michael LaFosse at the Origamido Studio.
Approximately 2" x 3" (5 cm x 8 cm)
Wet-folded from handmade flax fiber paper.

Daniel Robinson's goal for the *Samurai Helmet Beetle* was to
generate all of the beetle's appendages of the appropriate length,
arranged in their proper location, while not generating superfluous
creases. Designing and folding accurate and lifelike origami insects
is high on the list for many origami artists—not just for the challenge, but for the simple reason that of all possible natural history
subjects, few can match the arthropods in appropriateness of form.
Even live ones look folded!

Big Brown Bat, *Eptesicus fuscus*

Michael LaFosse
USA
Life-size; approximately 10" (25 cm) across the wings
Folded from a 10" (25 cm) square of kozo fiber paper
handmade by Michael LaFosse.

The artist had first set out to make the *Big Brown Bat* at the age of ten, and by age sixteen, he realized that to achieve the best effect, he should make the paper himself. The paper made for the bat is heavily sized and so it had to be wet-folded. Wetting the paper relaxes the sizing so that it may be more easily shaped, and slows the folding process down considerably. Once the paper is dry, the folds stay firmly in place. The bat was wet-folded to a certain stage, then left to dry completely. Later, selected areas were wet again for specialized work. This prevented deformation of the other areas of the bat. Usually this is accomplished over a period of several days.

Happy Good-Luck Bats

Michael LaFosse
USA
Roosting bats 1.5" x 2.75" (4 cm x 7 cm);
flying bats 2.5" x 4" (6 cm x 10 cm)
Wet-folded from diagonally bisected 5.5"
(14 cm) squares of heavy art paper.

The bats' triangular wings are cleanly represented by simple fan-folding, which also helps to form the three-dimensional body. Wings open and they are flying—closed, they can roost!

In China, the bat is revered as a symbol of good luck, largely because the Chinese words for *bat* and *good fortune* are homonyms. One often sees stylized versions of bats used ornamentally on ceramics, in tapestries, and in wood carvings. Five red bats amplify the good fortune, since the color red is considered lucky, and the number five represents the Five Happinesses. Inspired by the Chinese's happy interpretation of these animals, the artist playfully stylized this origami bat, which he most often folds in red paper.

Compare *Happy Good-Luck Bats* with *Big Brown Bat* (page 17) for a good idea of how an artist can use the versatility of origami, through style differences, to express a wide interpretation of a subject.

Rose

Toshikazu Kawasaki
Japan
Rose 2.5" x 2.5" (6 cm x 6 cm); leaf 3" x 3.25" (8 cm x 9 cm)
Rose folded from a square of Japanese tissue paper; each leaf triplet
folded from a square of dyed washi.

This modern origami flower design exhibits none of the hard, straight-line geometry typical
of traditional folded-paper models. Whereas most origami renditions of flowers are formed
with radial symmetry, Kawasaki wisely built his rose designs upon a spiral twist from the
paper's center. This twist forms four radial, multilayered walls of paper that can be gently
coaxed into a spiral-wrapped cylinder.

This cylinder, which resembles a rosebud, is gracefully formed, layer by layer, into a fully
bloomed rose. Four extensions of paper, left over from the forming of the petals, neatly cross
each other and cleverly lock the underside closed.

The leaf clusters are folded from single squares: each leaf is formed from one corner of the
paper, the stem from the fourth corner.

Rock Crystal

Toshikazu Kawasaki
Japan
Approximately 4" x 5" (10 cm x 13 cm)
Folded from multiple different-size squares of holographic mirrored mylar gift wrap.

Kawasaki's *Rock Crystal* is formed of two different units. The substrate, or base, is an intricately folded grid of multilayered peaks and valleys that form the attachment sizes for the crystal units. Each of the crystal spires is folded from squares of varying sizes. The top point of a crystal is the center of the square sheet. The four corners of each crystal element's square become the bottom of each spire, which fit neatly into attachment sites on the substrate's grid.

Modern methods and materials combine to form an inspired and convincing rendition of a classic work of nature. These crystal forms reflect of each other's mirrored surfaces, giving the illusion of crystal transparency. This is a multiunit or compound model construction, a relatively modern development in origami that is gaining in popularity and appreciation. It is an excellent example of the composition and ingenuity possible when using this method.

Clown Fish and Sea Anemone

J. C. Nolan
USA
3.5" x 6" (9 cm x 15 cm)
Folded from a 36" (91 cm) square of tissue foil.

The clown fish itself is generated by three points of paper that cluster in an outside corner. Since there are four such areas in the basic form, it is possible to have up to four fish swimming through the anemone.

J. C. Nolan was admiring clown fish in a pet store when he noticed that the light-colored stripes on these fish matched the color of the tentacles of the host anemone. This suggested the possibility of creating a color-change origami of the entire scene, for which he used a single sheet of paper—red on one side, white on the other. Nolan first designed a separate clown fish and then proceeded to incorporate this design into the folds of the anemone. This example of biological commensalism is profoundly exhibited in this model: the clown fish and sea anemone are truly one!

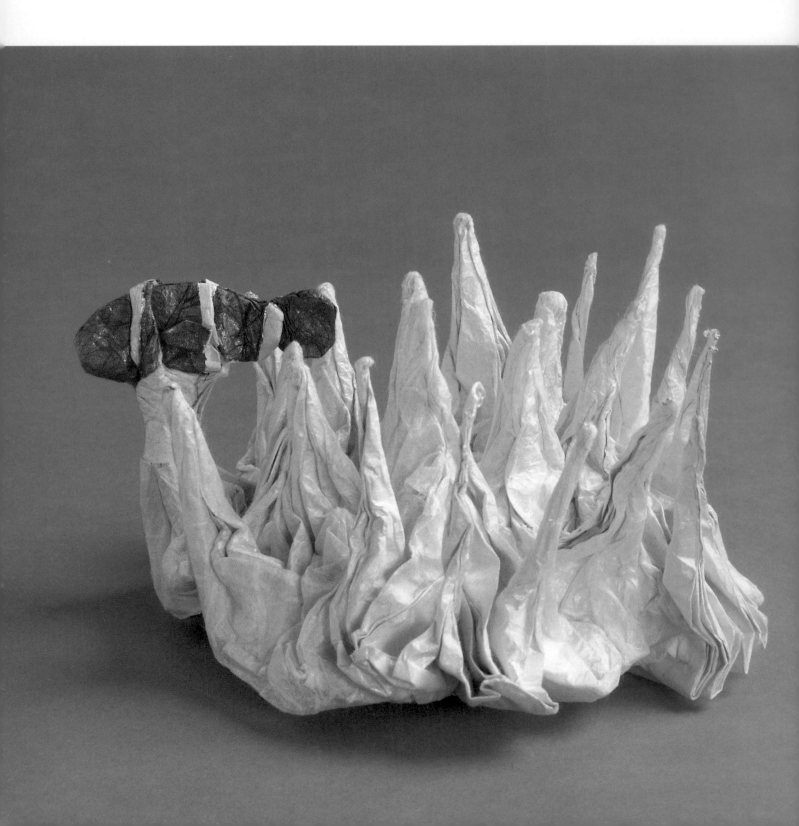

Fly

Alfredo Giunta
Italy
Life-size
Each is folded from two sheets of paper: the wings were made of transparent paper; the rest of the body was made of Japanese foil paper.

So tiny and detailed are these models that Giunta used tweezers to fold them. Alfredo is a serious student of natural subjects and his creations are full of life. These models, displayed in their handmade box have never been shown before. Giunta's method and choice of materials is so convincing that during the photography session, it was important to alert everyone that these "flies" were out of their boxes and that no one was to swat any any such creature without a careful inspection first.

Three-Headed Dragon

John Montroll
USA
Approximately 5" x 10" (13 cm x 25 cm)
Folded from an 18" (46 cm) square of Canson art paper

It is often difficult for the uninitiated to believe that a paper sculpture can be created from folding a single square of paper without the use of scissors. In this three-headed dragon, the three heads and the tail are each formed from one of the corners of the paper, making four legs and two wings, while allowing such long extensions for each neck.

Stegosaurus

Fumiaki Kawahata
Japan
Approximately 6" x 12" (15 cm x 30 cm)
Folded from a 23.5" (60 cm) square of Japanese origami-type paper.

Fumiaki Kawahata has written an entire book on his origami dinosaurs. He creates the characteristic back plates of the *Stegosaurus* from an elegant series of box pleats that are installed in the earliest stages of folding. The scale of the pleats is graduated so that various sizes of back plates are appropriately formed.

There are simpler methods, however, as in the case of Joseph Wu's one-fold stegosaurus. To observe this technique firsthand, fold a square sheet of paper in half, roughly in diagonal fashion, so that all four corners of the paper are equally spaced and are in an arch, thus representing the stegosaurus' back (see illustration below).

Elephant and Rabbit

Joseph Wu
Canada
Each approximately 5.5" (14 cm) tall
Elephant folded from a denim blend paper; rabbit folded from a cotton
Kraft and straw blend paper; both handmade by Reg Lissel of Vancouver.

Fully three-dimensional, both models feature closed backs and bellies. The techniques used in each are quite
different, though. The elephant cocks his head to one side, testifying to a twist in the paper at the neck.
Joseph Wu formed the full body by locking each side. The rabbit is closed down the back and up the front.
These techniques are becoming more familiar as designers share their approaches with one another.

Wu credits David Brill and Herman Van Goubergen (both featured in this book) with pioneering the ideas of
the elephant's construction, using the inherent tension of the fold-to-hold, a three-dimensional fullness without wet-folding. He designed the rabbit specifically for 1999, the Year of the Rabbit.

Rhinoceros

Edwin Corrie
Switzerland
4" x 7.5" (10 cm x 19 cm)
Folded from an A4 format
(silver rectangle) of handmade paper.

The folds of this rhino use clean divisions of the 90-degree angle—67.5, 45, 22.5, etc.—and so they are harmonious and reliably generated. The line of the back, from nose to tail, has an expressive posture.

All of Corrie's origami animals posses a playful personality, which is engaging and often humorous. Anyone familiar with even a few of his creations can easily pick a Corrie model out of a crowd. His models are so wonderfully engineered that anyone who folds the pattern with moderate care will reproduce a fine example of the design. To many, realizing this high level of refinement and elegance is the epitome of the art of origami design.

Desert Scorpion and Praying Mantis

Michael LaFosse
USA
Life-size
Each folded from a square of paper and with no cutting;
papers handmade by Michael LaFosse.

As 1997 Resident Artist with the Arizona-Sonora Desert Museum (ASDM) in Tucson, the author lived with the animals and plants for a month before making special paper from desert plant fibers and designing origami renditions for his masterful origami exhibit *Animals of the Sonora Desert* at the ASDM's Ironwood Gallery in 1998. The *Desert Scorpion* came out of that experience; the *Praying Mantis* is from the author's back yard.

Tyrannosaurus Rex Skeleton

Issei Yoshino
Japan
Designed by Issei Yoshino
7" x 12.5" (18 cm x 32 cm)
Folded from tie-dyed washi by Masao Hatori.

Yoshino's magnificent *Tyrannosaurus Rex Skeleton* promoted a new respect for compound origami models. His "mane" fold, as shown in his horse on the following page, is distinctive and elegant, and broke new ground in origami style and technology. It insists that the mane is an important and commanding feature of the horse and so the arching pleats are literally central to this design. Likewise, the geometric, diamond-shaped scales that form the back of Yoshino's *Wild Boar* (also on the following page) are important; it's as if the rest of the boar was designed around this prominent feature. Issei Yoshino's designs have inspired and influenced thousands, despite his short life of only thirty-one years. These examples of Yoshino's origami designs were folded by Masao Hatori, one of Japan's finest folders.

Horse and Wild Boar

Designed by Issei Yoshino
Horse 4" x 7" (10 cm x 18 cm);
Wild Boar 3" x 6" (8 cm x 15 cm)
Folded from tie-dyed washi by Masao Hatori.

Allosaurus Skeleton BELOW AND FOLLOWING PAGES

Robert Lang
USA
Approximately 35.5" x 12" (90 cm x 30 cm)
Wet-folded from sixteen 13.8" (35 cm) squares of "elephant hide" paper.

The impressive skull of the *Allosaurus Skeleton* is composed of only three pieces of paper. Lang's choice of paper adds
to the effect: its hard, smooth surface and fossil-like color are quite convincing, and the way in which Lang posed this
composition conveys a lifelike sense of animation that one expects to see in modern dinosaur mounts.

Bison

Akira Yoshizawa
Japan
Large bison is approximately 13" x 7.5" (33 cm x 19.05 cm)
Each is folded from a single square sheet of heavy, colored art paper.

These massive, yet gentle, animals of the North American plains have been folded in the inimitable style that Akira Yoshizawa is revered for. There is an important difference between the "lifelike" and "realistic" in origami, and these wet-folded bison certainly fall into the lifelike category. All of the best examples of origami renditions of living things must express a spirit of the living character, whether they are super-realistic, semi-realistic, mildly abstract, or severely abstract; there is nothing more realistic than a taxidermy specimen, but how lifeless it can appear.

Field of Roses

Toshikazu Kawasaki
Japan
Approximately 5" (12.70 cm) square
From a single 17" (43 cm) square sheet of Japanese washi covered, paper-backed foil.

Each of the thirty-six rosebuds echoes a spiral rhythm and is in lovely harmony with the paper itself. The foundation of this paper-folding technique is a grid of squares; imposed upon each square element is a twist, and each arm of a twist gracefully leads into and out of the neighboring buds. In this compact form the buds are tight together and waiting to bloom. Pull open the form and an expanding surface of intertwining spiral forms appears.

Tiger

Hideo Komatsu
Japan
Approximately 10" (25 cm) long
Folded from a square of paper-backed foil, colored differently on each side.

Here is an impressive example of inside-out origami, which is arguably the finest single-sheet origami tiger method known today. Previously, many origami artists used black and orange striped paper from which to fold tigers, or they painted the stripes on later. Komatsu's *Tiger* uses John Montroll's breakthrough inside-out technique for producing stripes and spots on animals, such as zebras, spotted cows, and giraffes. Developed only recently, this origami tiger appeared in time to help celebrate 1998, the Chinese Year of the Tiger.

A series of overlapping paper layers are developed on the outside of the model. These layers are somewhat open so that they display the inside surface of the paper, which is of a different color than the outside layer—thus inside-out origami.

Hideo credits the influence of Seiji Nishikawa's origami tiger for part of the development of this tiger's face.

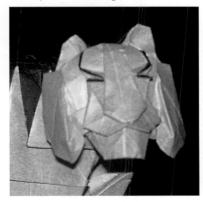

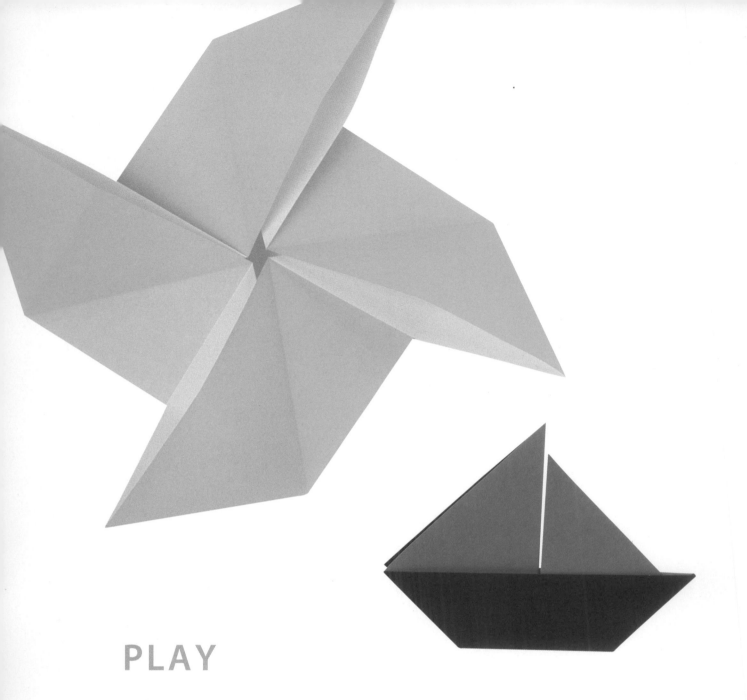

PLAY

Origami artists, in any idle moment, can amuse themselves and anybody nearby with a piece of paper, perhaps improvising a simple paper airplane or other toy. This scenario plays itself out many thousands of times a day throughout the world, in homes, in schoolyards, and at work. The classic and time-honored origami toys that have been passed down for generations are simple and easy to remember and teach. That's why they have survived and proliferated.

Today, there are thousands of new origami toys. Many in this section, like Jeff Beynon's Spring Into Action and John Montroll's Chessboard and Pieces, are engineering marvels—anything but child's play. Others, like Soon Young Lee's Talking Lips, are simple enough for most people to remember after a little practice.

This sailboat, which is the logo for OrigamiUSA, looks as if it were folded from two, differently colored sheets of paper, but, in fact, it is made from a single sheet of paper that is colored differently on each side. The bottom of the sailboat is an L-shaped form that allows the boat to stand upright on a flat surface: blow on the sails and it glides to victory in a tabletop race. The pinwheel, or windmill, is not only a toy, but is also a very important starting form for many classic origami models, such as the Pajarita on page 49.

Pinwheels and Sailboats

Folded by Michael La Fosse
Range in size from 2" to 4" (5.08 cm to 10.16 cm)
Folded from single squares of origami paper.

Jumping Frog

Tomoko Fuse
Japan
Approximately 4" (10 cm) long
Folded from a 7" (18 cm) square of coated Kraft paper.

There are numerous versions of the jumping frog that range from a simple, modern version best folded from index cards to the fairly complex, traditional Japanese inflatable frog, which has been folded for hundreds of years.

Tomoko Fuse's origami frog is relatively simple with satisfyingly lifelike detail; it's a good jumper, too. All origami jumping frogs have one thing in common: a concentration of folded paper under the rump, which when pressed firmly at the back edge will spring away like tiddlywinks. For this reason, papers that are relatively thick for their size should be used when folding any jumping origami model. Also, smaller models generally perform better than larger ones.

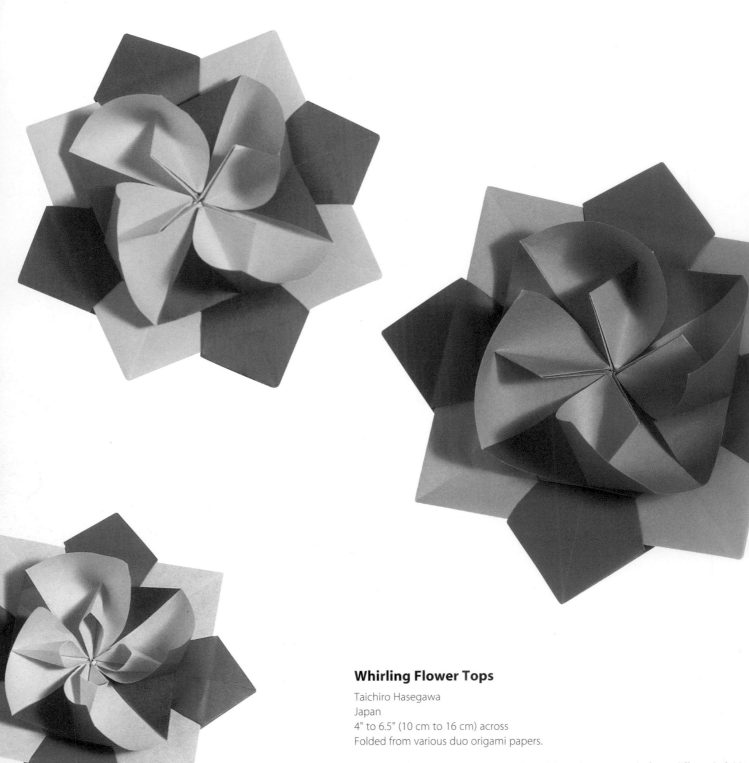

Whirling Flower Tops

Taichiro Hasegawa
Japan
4" to 6.5" (10 cm to 16 cm) across
Folded from various duo origami papers.

These tops are compound models each composed of two differently folded
pieces of paper, and both papers are square and of equal size. The corners of the
top flower securely fit into pockets of the base. Since both sides of the paper
show on each folded element, there may be up to four colors if each side of the
two papers used are differently colored. This origami can also be used as an
elegant package bow or ornament. To make the tops spin, place on any smooth,
flat surface and blow straight down into the center of the flower.

Pajarita

Traditional, Spain
Approximately 6" x 6" (15.24 cm)
Folded from a single, 8.5" (21.59 cm) square of colored offset paper.

In Spanish, a pajarita is a small bird. It is also the name given by the Spanish to this simple folded model. This paper toy can be traced back to the end of the eighteenth century and has been adopted as a logo by the Asociación Española de Papiroflexia. So abstract a design, it evokes different images to different people: horse, crow, parrot, dog, seal, and, of course, bird.

The folding method has much in common with many of the early paper folding designs credited to the Chinese, most notably the pinwheel. As with so many of the early Chinese folds, the square of paper for folding these models is divided into a grid of smaller squares.

Winged Hearts

Francis Ow
Singapore
2.5" x 4.5" (6 cm x 11 cm)
Each folded from single squares of duo origami paper
(in this case, one side is pink and the other side is magenta).

These winged hearts were made by folding two corners to the center of a square piece of paper to make an upside-down house shape. The "roof" was then folded to become the heart, and the remaining two corners of the square became the pleated wings. Bringing those two corners to the center exposed the other side of the paper, which is of a different color, so this delightful valentine has wings differntly colored than the heart.

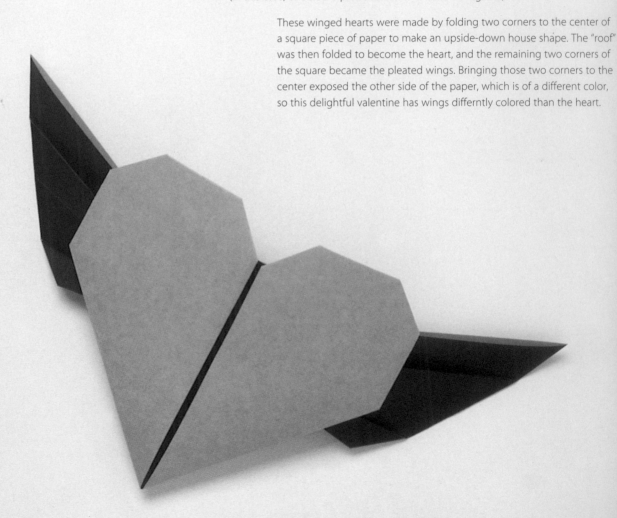

Spring into Action

Jeff Beynon
UK
Extended, 8" (20 cm) long; collapsed, 2" (5 cm) in diameter
Folded from 15:8 ratio rectangular sheets of colored bond paper.

An internationally recognized modern classic, *Spring into Action* is a real finger-twister! The actual crease pattern for this model is simple enough to generate a regular grid of diagonally bisected rectangles, which can easily be pleated or scored into the paper. The challenge is to manipulate the sheet into a helical, twisted, collapsible cylinder. Some beginners take more than an hour to do this; however, practice and patience bring rich rewards. There is nothing like the thrill of exercising your first completed example of this excellent model—a true feat of folded-paper action engineering.

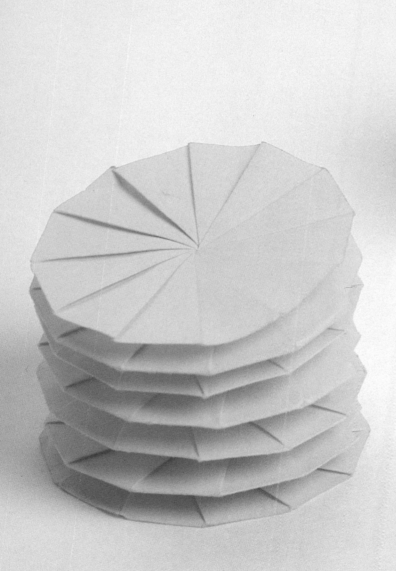

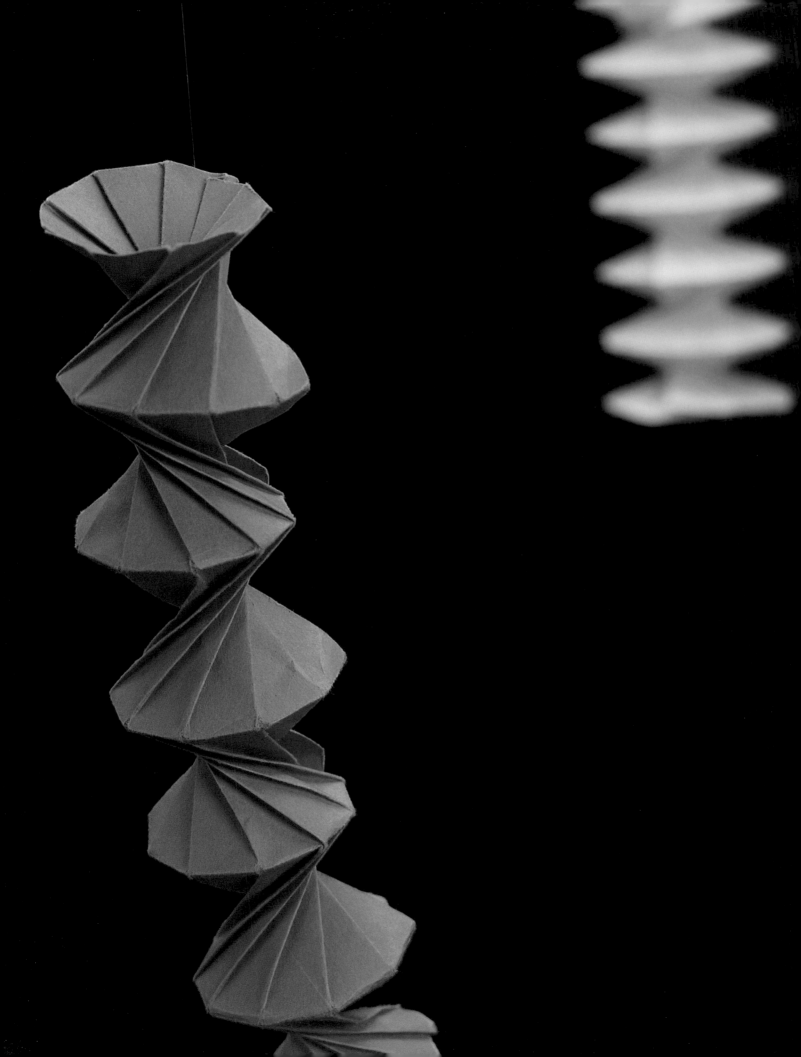

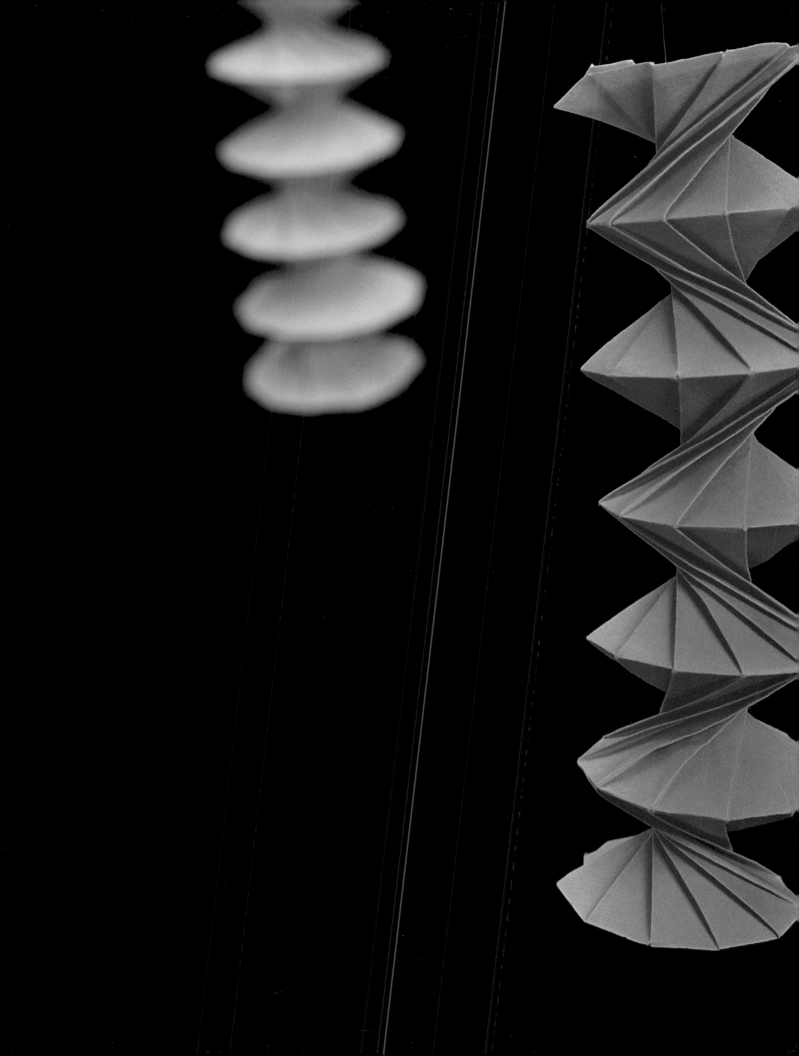

Aerogami™

Michael LaFosse
USA
Approximately 6" (15 cm)
Folded from single sheets of origami paper.

The elements that go into making a pure origami airplane design are simple: one sheet of paper, no cutting, no paste, and no tape. The models should be elegant and satisfying to fold, but they must also fly well. Pictured are a few of the author's personal favorites from his own extensive line of original designs. The diagrams for folding the *Flying Fox* seen here can be found on pages 130–133. Most of his airplanes feature locking folds and have user-friendly, adjustable flight control surfaces such as spoilers, flaps, and rudders, which add a touch of style to the design.

America's Paper Cup®

Eric Joisel
France
10" x 30" (25 cm x 76 cm)
Folded from five pieces of "elephant hide" paper; cup body folded from a compound sheet approximately 27" x 55" (70 cm x 140 cm).

Most of the construction of the trophy is standard fan-pleating, but what pleating! The elegant shape of the main body was tastefully formed by reversing the direction of the pleats—outward for wide and inward for narrow. The length and angle of these folds determine final proportion and shape. Once all of the pleats have been installed in the sheet, the two opposite sides of the paper are brought together and joined, thus forming the round shape of the cup. Fixtures, such as the spout and the handle, were folded from separate pieces of paper and added later. The trophy was specially created for the America's Paper Cup® championship paper boat race, the first of which was held during the Third Southeastern Origami Festival (SEOF) in Charlotte, North Carolina.

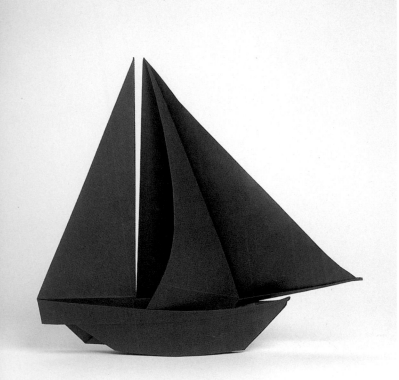

Sailing Yacht

Gérard Ty Sovan
Cambodia/France
12" x 13.5" (30 cm x 34 cm)
Folded from a 27" (69 cm) square of tinted Kraft paper.

Gérard Ty Sovan's method of designing sailing ships is remarkable for two reasons: his ships are among the most realistic and elegant in the origami repertoire, and they are created from the blintzed bird base—a double-layered version of the folding form used to create the famous Japanese crane.

Today, there are perhaps hundreds of origami boats to choose from. Some, like this beautiful sailing yacht, are strictly ornamental, while other versions may be floated on water for a vicarious journey.

Chessboard and Pieces

John Montroll
USA

Chessboard 2" tall x 6" square (5 cm x 15 cm), folded from a 27" (69 cm) square of coated Kraft paper that is black on one side and natural on the other; pieces range from 2.25" to 3.5" (6 cm to 9 cm) tall, each with 1" base (3 cm), folded from 6" (15 cm) squares of heavy colored Kraft paper.

As contributors to the advancement of origami continue to apply their wits to the outstanding challenges in the area of the single uncut square sheet of paper, the seemingly impossible becomes possible. There have been many attempts at designing an inside-out single-sheet origami chessboard by paperfolders, and most have partly realized their goals by folding square fractions of a board and then assembling (the modular method).

John Montroll's folding method is direct; the model's many layers are symmetrical, making it well balanced and neat. Montroll is an avid and formidable chess player, and he has also designed a full set of chess pieces with which to play.

Tops

Akira Yoshizawa
Japan
Approximately 2" (5.08 cm) to 4" (10.16 cm) across.
Folded from single sheets of various papers.

Akira Yoshizawa has designed scores of tops. For him, each must maintain its spin for over one minute to be considered a successful design.

From simple to complex, there is great variety of technique and design represented in this collection. However, for most of these tops, Mr. Yoshizawa developed the spindle from the corners of the paper and the focal spinning point from the center of the paper.

Talking Lips

Soon Young Lee
South Korea
Approximately 3" x 3" (8 cm x 8 cm)
Each folded from a 6" (15 cm) square of duo origami paper.

Just when you think that all of the good "simple" origami models have already been discovered, something like this comes along and reminds you to keep looking. *Talking Lips* is a delightful combination of two classic origami categories: inside-out origami and action origami.

These are inside-out because the color of the inside of the paper is turned out to color the lips, and action because pulling on the corners makes the lips open and close. With kind permission, Soon Young Lee's method for folding these paper lips is included on page 126–127.

Matrioshka Dolls

Luda Lezhneva
Russia
2.5" x 4.5" to 4.5" x 8.5" (6 cm x 11 cm to 11 cm x 22 cm)
Folded from Japanese Yuzen papers.

Wooden Matrioshka dolls are inextricably linked to Russian folk art and culture, so it is appropriate that these nesting dolls were created from the hands of a Russian origami artist. Interestingly, the first Matrioshka dolls were made to resemble a Japanese character named Fukuruma, and were originally from the island of Honshu. They appeared in Russia around 1890.

Both the top and bottom elements are folded from the same form, the preliminary base, which is essentially a simple pleated bag or umbrella shape. The sides and closed ends are shaped with simple folds that also prevent the umbrellalike layers from spreading open. In final form, the top fits neatly into the bottom; smaller dolls fit into larger ones in practically the same fashion as their wooden counterparts.

Butterfly Ball

Kenneth Kawamura
USA
Each assembled from twelve identically shaped elements, formed by three simple folds placed into 3.5" (9 cm) squares of colored offset papers.

Kenneth Kawamura credits his friend Joseph R. Power with planting the seed for this design. One day, Power showed Kawamura an interesting modular origami construction that resembled an octahedron with sunken faces. The six units used in this construction were the familiar waterbomb base, which Kawamura began to regard with new possibilities as he mentally made some connections of his own. Later, Kawamura would pursue these possibilities, developing a series of multiunit polyhedra, one of which ultimately became known as the *Butterfly Ball,* a great contribution to the repertoire of puzzle and action origami pieces. It is as much fun to take apart as it is to put together: toss the ball into the air and strike it sharply from beneath as it descends for a shower of origami butterflies.

It also makes an appropriate party favor for New Year's: there are twelve units, one for each month of the past year. At the end of the countdown, guests explode their Butterfly Balls and grab one piece out of the air. Each of the twelve pieces has a different New Year's resolution (or fortune) written on it.

FORM AND FUNCTION

The models in this section demonstrate a wide range of origami design. They evoke words such as *humor* and *beauty* as well as *ingenuity* and *practicality*. For many, origami's greatest appeal is the magic of transformation. Many examples of this can be found in this section, which showcases the union of form and function in origami design and features some of the most exquisite examples of geometric origami designs. These exquisitely folded modular structures are a feast of colors, forms, patterns, and shadows.

Consider Valerie Vann's *Magic Rose Cube,* an innocent-looking paper cube that, when coaxed in the right places, blooms into a stunning paper rose blossom. Or the origami box construction methods of Tomoko Fuse and Chris Palmer, which can turn even ordinary newspaper into extraordinary and elegant packages for gifts.

In the spirit of beauty and usefulness are David Petty's inspired modular wreaths and rings. Each is composed of multiple identical folded paper units. One part of a unit fits neatly into a pocket of another. When the specified number of units has been properly joined, a colorful wreath is formed. No glue is required to hold the units together, and there are endless possibilities when variations in paper size, color, and pattern are considered and implemented. It is also possible to fold these wreaths from stiffened fabrics.

Wreaths and Rings

David Petty
United Kingdom
Approximately 3" to 8" (8 cm to 20 cm) across
Folded from multiple square sheets of commercial
and Zenacraf origami papers.

Boxes

Tomoko Fuse
Japan
Each 2" deep x 5" across (5 cm x 13 cm)
Folded from a variety of silk-screened Japanese Yuzen papers.

Few things show paper's intrinsic beauty as well as Tomoko Fuse's *Boxes*. The geometry for each box is inherent in the folding method—no special measuring or marking tools are needed. Each half of a box is composed of several sheets of folded paper that cleverly lock together to form a neat container.

Five-Intersecting Tetraheda FOLLOWING PAGES

Tom Hull
USA
11" (28 cm) in diameter
Folded from thirty pieces of Canford artist paper.

This stunning modular composition was inspired by a poster image of a five-intersecting tetrahedra, a geometric form composed of five four-sided intersecting pyramids. Professor Tom Hull perceived the five tetrahedra as frames that could be interwoven. He found the perfect solution for his frame construction in Francis Ow's *60-Degree Unit*, six of which neatly lock together to form a tetrahedral frame. Next, Hull had to determine the ideal proportions of the paper: too wide and the frames wouldn't weave; too narrow and the woven forms would be loose. Ultimately, he determined that the units could be most effectively folded from 1" x 3.2" (3 cm x 8 cm) rectangles. Each tetrahedral frame is easy to construct, but the interweaving of the five forms presents an exciting mental challenge.

Pentagon Box with Pentagonal Star Flower Tower

Chris Palmer
USA
Box approximately 10" (25 cm) across;
Flower tower approximately 8" (20 cm) across
Each flower tower folded from a sheet of "elephant hide" paper.

Chris Palmer has adapted many of his twist forms and flower towers to origami box design, and to great effect. Here, Palmer has created an unusual pentagonal box shape: the lid and the bottom are each folded from a single sheet of paper. In the box is an example of one of his beautiful flower towers, folded from a single ten-sided sheet of paper.

These days there are hundreds of origami boxes to learn about and to fold. The utilitarian, practical side of this area of origami is appealing in many ways. For one, paper is a common, often highly decorated material that is easy to work with. Also, origami boxes make wonderful containers for gift giving. Practicality aside, the rich invention and architectural beauty of such origami boxes are awesome. The graceful lines and clean panels of such folding have the power to elevate even the humblest of papers.

Magic Rose Cube

Valerie Vann
USA
Closed, 2.25" (6 cm) across; open, 6.5" (17 cm) across
Folded from six 5.87" (15 cm) squares of colored Kraft paper.

Appropriately named, the *Magic Rose Cube* converts from a tidy cube to a rose blossom in full bloom by the gentle pulling or twisting of the cleverly engineered layers of paper on the cube's surface. Three of the faces of the cube open to form the head of the flower, and the remaining three faces open to form the green leaves of the calyx. Designed in 1995, this spectacular modular origami model quickly made its way around the world the time-honored way: by one person enthusiastically teaching another.

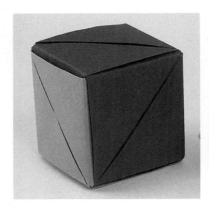 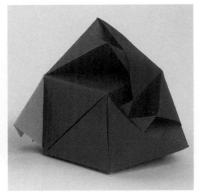

Spires

Tomoko Fuse
Japan
Approximately 9" (23 cm) tall
Folded from single squares of paper.

Looking like pine trees or mountain peaks from some strange fractal landscape, these faceted, folded paper spires are commanding in any scale. A pleasing aspect of this work is the way in which the eye is treated to a varying display of the paper's surface through light and shadow and repeated, but differently sized, triangular panels.

Tomoko Fuse's method is wonderfully direct: a square of paper is radial pleated from one corner to form a long, narrow spear. This spear is folded into a flat spiral, which will install the facet creases. The paper is then opened fully, formed into a cone, and each facet is properly set.

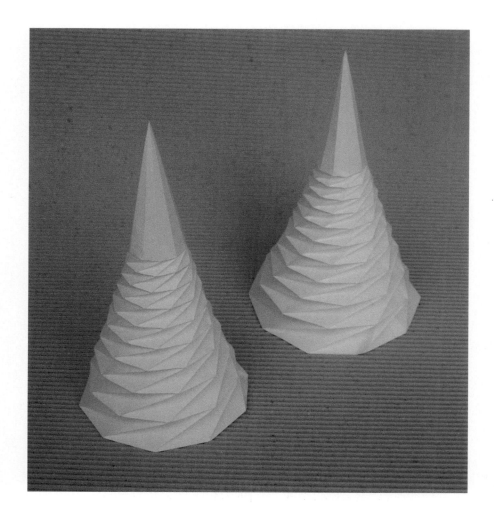

Abstract ABOVE AND FOLLOWING PAGES

Paul Jackson
United Kingdom
Approximately 4" x 6" (10 cm x 15 cm)
Folded from a sheet of watercolor paper hand-colored with dappled washes
of acrylic paint.

This form is produced by fan-folding a graduate-pleated sheet of paper, then shaping the pleats by pulling to arch the ribs. Once shaped, the faces of the arches are brought together, closing the form. Glue is not necessary to keep the form closed.

Many variations of this design are possible, such as spheres, cylinders, and open bowls, to name a few. Variations in the size and number of the pleats, as well as their direction of overlap, contribute to an infinite range of subtlety. Paul Jackson has applied charcoal, color pencil, pastel, and paint to the surface of his papers before folding. Such decorative pretreatment of the paper is unusual in origami and brings the paper's surface to life.

Black Forest Clock

Robert Lang
USA
Approximately 35.5" x 12" (90 cm x 30 cm)
Wet-folded from sixteen 13.8" (35 cm) squares of "elephant hide" paper.

Some years ago, Robert Lang set out to design an origami grandfather clock with a ticking pendulum whose swing would be actuated by gently squeezing the clock case. Due to numerous failed attempts, Lang decided to take another road and the *Black Forest Clock* was born.

This clock is one of the great masterpieces of single-sheet, rectangle-form origami, and is a very demanding model to make. To date, only two display examples exist, both folded by Lang, and there are no diagrams available to learn how to fold this clock. This surely is one of those origami models that compels the viewer to imagine how it could be done—it seems an impossibility! It should be admired for its technical brilliance, but not at the expense of its beauty, and Lang assures that it keeps excellent time exactly twice a day.

Chinese Teapot and Cups FOLLOWING PAGES

Sy Chen
China/USA
Teapot 4" x 8.5" (10 cm x 22 cm); cups each 1.5" x 2" (4 cm x 5 cm)
Wet-folded from Canson art paper.

The teapot model was designed by Sy Chen in 1996 and was one of his first designs to fulfill his dream of representing aspects of Chinese life in his art. The cups were designed at a later date to accompany the pot in their appearance in Dorothy Englman's short film *Folding California*. Chen's choice of paper gives these models a potterylike look.

Although the Chinese are credited with the discovery of paper and have been working with folded-paper design longer than anyone, Chinese folded paper objects are scarcely represented in the repertoire. This exquisite Chinese tea set hints at what has been missing.

Paper Fastening Flower and Envelope

Gay Merrill Gross
USA
Paper Fastening Flower: 1.75" x 3" (4 cm x 8 cm), folded from two
3.5" (9 cm) squares of colored offset paper; envelope: 5" x 7" (13 cm x 18 cm), folded from a
10" (25 cm) square of decorative Japanese paper.

There are many uses for this easy-to-fold, easy-to-remember design. Gay Merrill
Gross herself not only uses this origami model to fasten papers and seal
envelopes, she also uses it as a button cover. The diagrams for folding this model
appear on page 122 to 125.

Waiting For a Friend

Akira Yoshizawa
Japan
Approximately 10" (25.40 cm) tall
Folded from a single square of back-coated Japanese paper.

Inspired by the experimentation of the modern abstract expressionists, Akira Yoshizawa has been creating abstract origami for over fifty years. This piece is one of a series by Yoshizawa representing the images through the figure of birds, wet-folded from relatively thick paper. There are elements of folding that are almost classic (Japanese origami style) in their folding—and by this virtue rather abstract—but the long, lyrical, and ascending sweep in the paper is very modern.

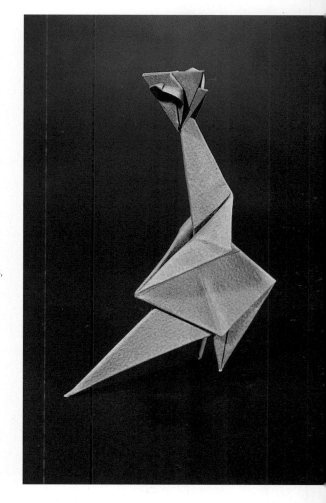

Geometric Composition OPPOSITE

Ethan Plaut
USA
Approximately 4" x 8" x 8" (10 cm x 20 cm x 20 cm)
Folded from a square of machine-made artist paper.

Geometric Composition is one in a series of folded compositions that Ethan Plaut has based upon the crease pattern of the classic Japanese bird base, a familiar and powerful paperfolding base structure common to thousands of traditional and modern origami designs. This bird base pattern is folded, repeatedly, as a tiling formation. Because the bird base is a three-dimensional structure, it can transform a flat sheet into a domelike structure. The size and number of bird bases can be varied, as can the relative position of their component structures. From a seemingly simple set of variables comes rich potential for creativity. The composition pictured here is backlit, clearly showing the geometric intricacies of this type of work.

Landscape BELOW

Ethan Plaut
USA
Approximately 18" x 28" (46 cm x 71 cm)
Folded from an uncut rectangle of machine-made artist paper.

Ethan Plaut has explored the impact of using base patterns to affect changes in the topography of the entire folded nonrepresentational sheet here. He has begun in the center of the composition with an array of traditional bird base folds. He eventually adopts a more freestyle treatment, allowing the edges of the resulting landscape to revert to a more organic form. This piece features pleating to form curvilinear valleys, drumlins, and ridges. The net result is a pleasing yet unfamiliar place begging to be explored, if only by the eye. The soft- and hard-edged folds develop a rhythm in light and shadow, as found traditionally in a bas relief.

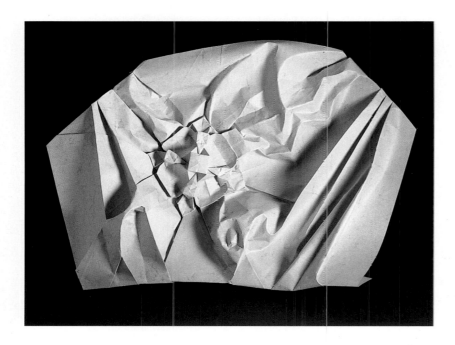

Bucky Ball OPPOSITE

Tom Hull
USA
Approximately 12" (30 cm) in diameter
Folded from 360 3" (8 cm) squares of origami paper.

Professor Tom Hull has created several interesting lessons and investigations around the pentagon-hexagon zigzag unit that composes this model. The name of the unit means you can make any polyhedron that is cubic (each corner of the polyhedron is a terminating point intersection of three edges) and is composed of only pentagonal and hexagonal faces. Many different structures are possible. Adding multiple colors expands the exercise into the territory of color mapping. How would you arrange a three-color collection of units in a 360-unit model so that no two units of the same color touch each other? In organic chemistry you can use these units to model C60 molecules, or Bucky Balls (and also Bucky Tubes), of different sizes. The diagrams for this model appear on pages 128 to 129.

Cosmosphere LEFT

Miyuki Kawamura
Japan
Approximately 23.5" in diameter (60 cm)
Folded from 1,890 3" (8 cm) square sheets of origami paper.

Miyuki Kawamura's *Cosmosphere* is an example of a monumental undertaking with stunning results in modular origami. The careful choice and arrangement of the different colors make this sculpture especially commanding.

Modular origami can consist of as few as two pieces of paper or as many as thousands. Often the folding of each unit is very simple. A single unit only hints at the potential of the finished model. Once assembled, the architectural beauty is at last revealed. It is hard to imagine that not long ago, multiunit origami was regarded by many as an inferior, even illegitimate origami.

Flower Tower Invitation

Chris Palmer
USA
Open, 7.5" (19 cm) across; closed, 3.5" (9 cm) in diameter
Folded from an octagonal piece of "elephant hide" paper.

To create these invitations, Chris Palmer composed the text elements in a computer graphics application to fit into the panels of his prescribed crease pattern. He then printed each sheet, cut the octagonal shape, and folded each by hand. These are the actual invitations from a showing of designer David Rodriguez's 1999 spring collection. Many of these fashions incorporated Palmer's incredible pleated designs. This exciting collaboration resulted in stunning outfits and groundbreaking use of Palmer's techniques.

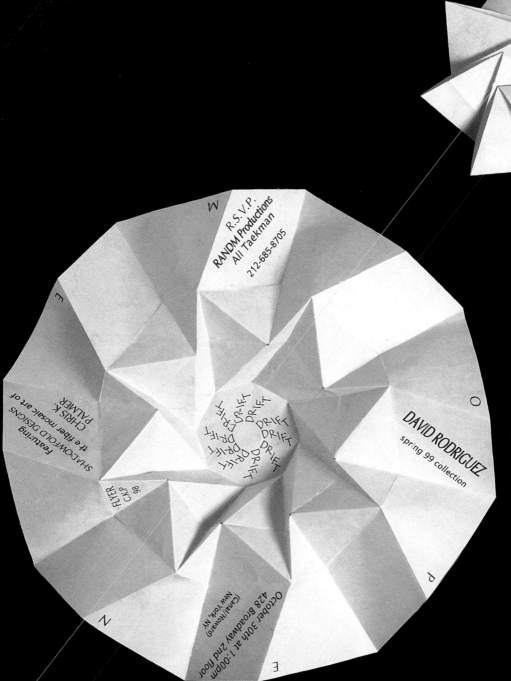

Flasher Hat

Jeremy Shafer
USA
Open, 24" (61 cm) in diameter; closed, 3" x 3.5" (8 cm x 9 cm)
Folded from a 27" (69 cm) square of Wynstone Marble paper.

The collapsible paper hat is a marvelous example of "flasher" technology, a fairly recent and delightful development in folding by Jeremy Shafer and Chris Palmer. Flashers are pleated twists that exhibit dynamic properties. Pull on opposite sides of a closed flasher and it will unwind in a faceted spiral maze; let go and it may pull itself shut again! Using this folding method, a large sheet of paper can be reduced to a compact cylinder about one-seventieth of its original area.

Buddha Mask

Akira Yoshizawa
Japan
Approximately 8" (20.32 cm) tall
Folded from a single square of gold-covered washi.

MASKS & FIGURES

IN THIS AREA OF PAPERFOLDING, AND PERHAPS MORE THAN IN THE other sections of this book, the observer gets a stronger personal sense of each artist. Sometimes the artist's cultural background may even be discernible in the finished piece. Eric Joisel's masks are unmistakably French, and the works of artists Akira Yoshizawa, Tomoko Fuse, Hojyo Takashi, and Satoshi Kamiya are full of the aesthetic hallmarks of Japan. Regardless of style or complexity, it is easy to relate to the humanesque. Wisdom and serenity are displayed in the features of this origami mask by Akira Yoshizawa, which uses relatively few folds to make its form. Yoshizawa's sensitive touch gently persuades the paper to form the lips of the mouth and the lids of the eyes. Mr. Yoshizawa asserts that the characteristics of the paper—color, texture, weight, foldability—have a psychological effect on the folder and so can inspire or defeat the project.

St. George and the Dragon

David Brill
United Kingdom
St. George: 7" x 8" (18 cm x 20 cm), folded from a square of decorative Kraft paper; spear folded from a rectangle of the same paper; horse folded from an equilateral triangle of backed Unryushi paper; shield folded from a square of commercial origami paper that is red on one side and white on the other.
Dragon: 4.5" x 5" (12 cm x 13 cm), folded from a square of washilike paper.

Creating a composition from origami-based elements can be quite an artistic challenge. Each element must be in scale and all materials should be carefully coordinated with regards to color and texture. The style of folding should be consistent throughout. A greater challenge still is the vital connection that each element must appear to have with each other, so gesture and placement are key. Here, St. George is intent on conquering the dragon, who seems to have been successfully caught unaware, while the horse ensures no chance of escape.

Divine Dragon

Satoshi Kamiya
Japan
8.5" x 16" (22 cm x 41 cm)
Folded from a 39" (1 m) square sheet of foil-backed washi.

Origami lends itself nicely to creating scales, horns, claws, and tails. In the *Divine Dragon*, each of the four limbs terminates in toes or fingers. There are also three formidable claws at the top of each wing.

Rendering such intricate detail necessitates using extremely thin paper with a certain degree of durability and compressibility. The artist chose to use a composite of lightweight Japanese paper bonded to aluminum foil. This two-layer material is relatively thin in proportion to the large area of the paper. The foil enables the composite to take and hold the shaping, yet can be compressed tightly where numerous layers accumulate bulk.

Three Masks ABOVE

Eric Joisel
France
Approximately 12" (30 cm) tall
Folded from single, 19" (50 cm) squares of French Kraft "Topsac," painted with acrylic paint (applied with a sponge), then varnished.

> Eric Joisel has developed this most plastic and efficient method for folding masks of the human face. Everyone who works with this method can truly add his or her own style. The nose is formed at the center of the square and from only one layer of paper in the mask; it is not a bulky technique. The result is three-dimensional, but rather simple. Joisel often paints the finished masks, adding a patina effect and creating a distinctive character.

Head of a Woman OPPOSITE

Eric Joisel
France
Approximately 9.5" x 12" (24 cm x 30 cm)
Wet-folded from a square of watercolor paper.

> This portrait is so wonderfully alive and perfect that numerous admirers of the piece have remarked that they know her. The delicate shaping of the nose and eyes is particularly winning. The technical use of the paper is economical, resulting in a hollow, masklike form with remarkably few overlapping layers. This freedom from bulkiness allows maximum potential for variation and expressiveness.

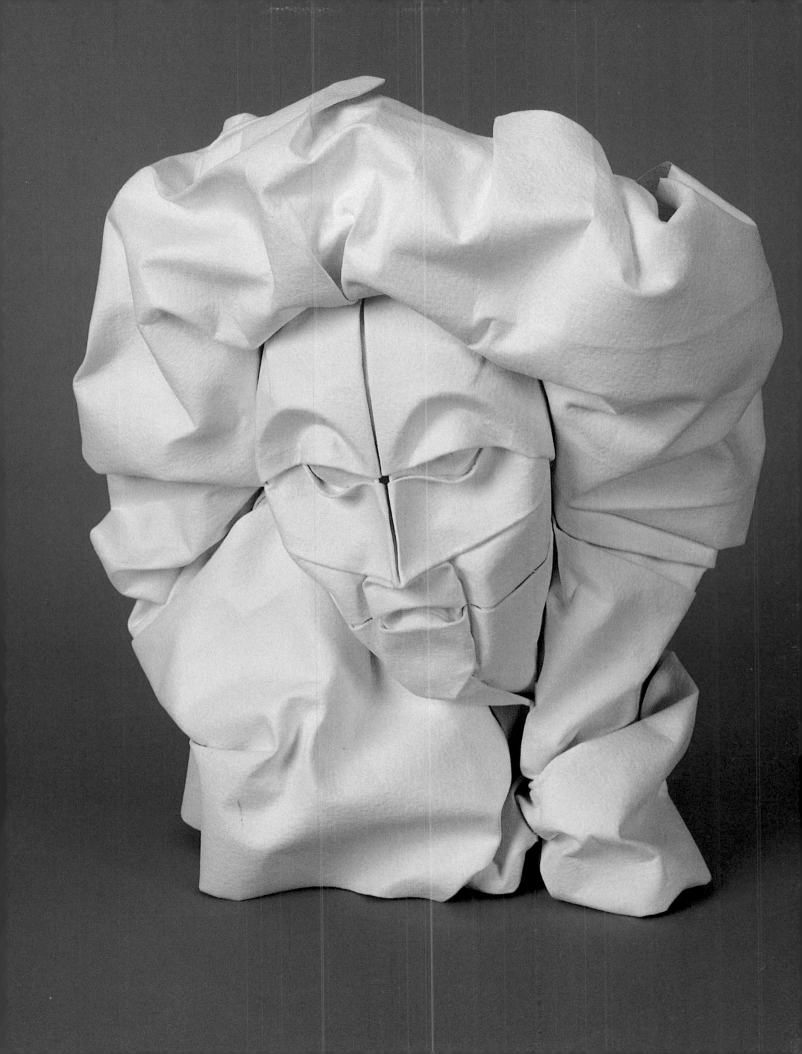

George L. Mountainlion

Michael LaFosse
USA
Approximately 6" x 8" (15 cm x 20 cm)
Folded from an 18" (46 cm) square of abaca, cotton, and agave blend
paper handmade by Michael LaFosse.

George L. Mountainlion was created for the author's 1998 one-man show at
Arizona-Sonara Desert Museum's (ASDM) Ironwood Gallery in Tucson, Arizona. The
museum wanted origami renditions of selected subjects: rattlesnakes, hummingbirds, coyotes, roadrunners, and cacti, to name a few. He not only designed and
folded the pieces, but also made special papers for each. Indigenous plant fibers
are part of these handmade papers, the qualities of which greatly add to the
borne-from-the-Sonora look and feel of the sculptures.

George L. Mountainlion is based on a mountain lion that lived at the ASDM in the
early 1950s. He was a mascot and an ambassador for the museum, and his likeness
is the museum's logo. The diagrams for this piece appear on pages 134 to 137.

Hannya

Tomoko Fuse
Japan
Approximately 8" (60 cm) tall
Folded from a single 23.5" (60 cm) square of two-sided washi.

Hannya is a famous Noh theater character who is a full-blown demon, created from jealousy, and who was once a woman. This origami rendition of the Noh mask has been made especially sinister with the photographer's stark lighting.

Tomoko Fuse carefully chooses and prepares papers for all of her origami art. For the *Hannya* mask, she pasted two sheets of washi together, one side red the other textured gold. The red side shows in the mouth. Such two-layered paste-ups of paper can hold expressive shaping well.

Fuse's authentic and expressive masks may surprise those who are only familiar with her geometric and modular work.

Chidou

Tomoko Fuse
Japan
Approximately 8" (20 cm) tall
Folded from a single 23.5" (60 cm) square of momigami.

Chidou is a character from early Japanese mythology, and one of Tomoko Fuse's favorites. The large ears, reminiscent of Buddha's, are typical of the earliest Japanese ceremonial and performance masks. Tomoko's rendering of Chidou captures his good and powerful nature.

Fuse's *Chidou* was wet-folded from specially prepared washi: two sheets pasted together, back-to-back, to give the paper substance and to preserve the softly folded features.

Maitreya

Hojyo Takashi
Japan
Approximately 7" (18 cm) tall
Folded from a single, 13.77" (35cm) square of paper.

Maitreya is the future Buddha in Buddhism. It is said that Maitreya will appear five billion, six hundred and seventy million years after Sakyamuni, the founder of Buddhism, died. Hojyo Takashi based this graceful origami model on a famous statue at Chugu-ji in Nara.

The folding method for this model is a blend of classical Japanese origami with the contemporary approach. The beginning folds are the basic folding form used to fold the traditional origami crane. With a little more preparation, the paper is fully opened and an elaborate pre-crease pattern is installed, moving a miniature copy of the crane base away from the center of the paper providing structure to fold the head in this area. This shift from center also proportions the limbs and the body. For most of the folding, this model is flat. The piece is finished with gracefull and sensitively formed curved folds that make it three-dimensional and bring it to life.

Shakyamuni

Akira Yoshizawa
Japan
Approximately 7" (17.78 cm) tall
Folded from a single square of handmade Kozo paper coated with
persimmon juice.

Shakyamuni is the great founder of Buddhism and an inspirational force for Akira Yoshizawa in his work. In his own words: "While living in this world, we have direct or indirect relationships—even with others who seem to be irrelevant—without noticing. I have learned my way of life by depending on the ideas of Shakyamuni. This work represents my thoughts about life."

Ohinasama LEFT

Makoto Yamaguchi
Japan
Folded from squares of washi. Flowers arranged by Mami Kawasak.

In Japan, the third of March is Girl's Festival Day, and these two dolls, representing a prince and princess, are the classic symbols for this special day. Usually the dolls are elaborately made and dressed in fine fabrics. A special gift of such dolls is made to young girls in Japan at some time in their life.

This composition is a special collaboration using the origami of Mr. Yamaguchi, of the Gallery Origami House, Tokyo, and a flower arrangement by one of Japan's leading ikebana artists, Mami Kawasak.

Labyrinth Walker BELOW AND FOLLOWING PAGES

Jeremy Shafer
USA
Approximately 8.5" wide x 10" tall (22 cm x 25 cm)
Folded from a 19.5" (50 cm) square of Wynstone Marble paper.

Jeremy Shafer modeled his design upon the Christian labyrinth, which is traditionally circular and is found in many churches around the world. He has neatly adapted this design to origami's tradition, the square. The maze pattern s creased into the sheet as a series of mountain-and-valley folds and then collapsed inward to form the stick-figure that Jeremy calls a labyrinth walker. Usually one walks around inside a labyrinth, but here it is the labyrinth itself that walks around. Each corner of the square becomes a limb, and the head of the labyrinth walker is formed at the middle of one of the square's edges.

Skull

Herman Van Goubergen
Belgium
Approximately 3" tall x 4" wide (8 cm by 10 cm)
Folded from an 8" (21 cm) square of "elephant hide" paper.

The apparently full frontal view of a human skull in this model is only possible with the aid of a mirror. Herman Van Goubergen began his idea for this piece with the understanding that a mirror image was usually the mirror twin of the real object but not necessarily so. There can be a considerable difference between the two images when your viewing angle changes. He decided to illustrate this by creating an object that, when placed upon a mirror, had a reflection very different from the apparent, real object. Looking for a likely subject, Van Goubergen decided to make some kind of a face. Further, he mused that the subject matter should have some connection with the concept: "Mirror; optical illusions; mystery; magic mirrors; black magic; skull. So, it just had to be a skull!"

This cleverly designed model comprises the crown and eye sockets of the skull. Inside the crown, and facing the surface of the mirror, are the nose, teeth, and lower jaw, which you see reflected in the mirror, thus completing the image.

Untitled Cubist Composition

Ethan Plaut
USA
Approximately 9" x 17" (23 cm x 43 cm)
Folded from four uncut 8.5" x 11" (22 cm x 28 cm) photocopies of text,
numbers, sheet music, and the *Mona Lisa*.

A collage of a face composed of folded sheets of text, sheet music, and photos, this work falls on both sides of the fence separating art and craft. It challenges the perception that if it's art, it can't be origami and vice versa. Plaut chose symbols of music, painting, and mathematics to become a visual amalgam of expression's common tools.

DIAGRAMS

ONE OF THE MOST SIGNIFICANT CONTRIBUTIONS TO ORIGAMI THIS CENTURY HAS UNDENIABLY been the development and adoption of a standardized, written language. Just as in music, an internationally accepted system of written symbols has allowed the art to flourish. This modern system for origami was developed by origami master Akira Yoshizawa of Japan. Trained in geometry and drafting, Yoshizawa created this system to help him document his prodigious output of origami designs—so he would not forget how to fold them. As his diagramming system began to be adopted, a few origami enthusiasts began to add their own symbols. Most notable of these early contributors was Samuel Randlett, and today we often refer to this language as the Yoshizawa/Randlett system.

One of the most brilliant features of Yoshizawa's original system was the concept of the mountain-fold line, indicated by double dots separating the dashes of the standard, dashed-line instruction to fold. It reduces the number of drawings required per model dramatically and so has helped to make the publishing of origami designs more space efficient. With the advent of the computer and the many easy-to-use graphics applications, the tedious task of diagramming origami models has been speeded up considerably. This has effectively improved the state-of-the-art by making the diagramming of even the most complex origami more possible.

In origami, just as in music, you will need some familiarity with the meaning of these symbols. Fold an example of the simple bookmark you'll find in the Key to Origami Symbols and Terms that follows to begin learning the meaning of mountain and valley folds, and the use of the most common arrows. Then proceed to the other projects; they are arranged progressively, easy to difficult. By doing these projects, you will see how simple and elegant this system is and you will pick it up quickly. Once you learn it, you will feel right at home using most any origami book. Here's a good tip: when following origami-diagrammed instructions, look ahead to the next step to see the form the paper will assume.

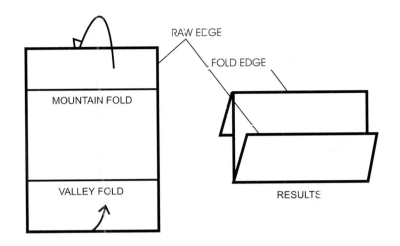

RAW EDGE

FOLD EDGE

MOUNTAIN FOLD

VALLEY FOLD

RESULTS

 IN FRONT

 BEHIND

 APPLY PRESSURE

 TURN MODEL OVER

 REPEAT PROCEDURE

VALLEY-FOLD

MOUNTAIN-FOLD

X-RAY VIEW

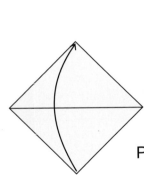

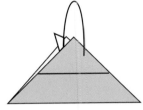

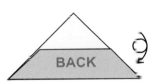 BACK

FRONT

Practice reading diagrams with this simple origami bookmark

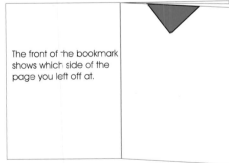

The front of the bookmark shows which side of the page you left off at.

Paper-Fastening Flower

Designed by Gay Merrill Gross
Diagrammed by Michael LaFosse

Here is a simple and clever design that you will find very useful. As a paper fastener it is decorative and strong. Wrap a card or small package in a square of paper and use this origami model to firmly seal in the contents. It makes a very distinctive impression.

For the flower and its leaf use three-to-four inch (7.62-to-10.16 cm) squares brightly colored off-set paper. Use any suitably decorative paper for your envelope.

FLOWER

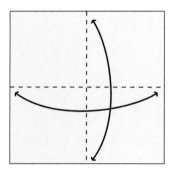

1 To begin flower, valley-fold and unfold the paper in half, edge-to-edge, both possible ways.

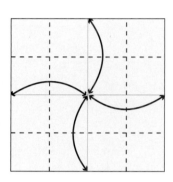

2 Valley-fold and unfold each of the four edges of the square to the center line. Turn the paper over.

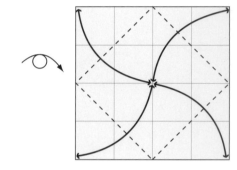

3 Valley-fold and unfold each of the corners of the square to the center.

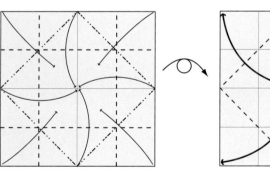

4 Turn the paper over.

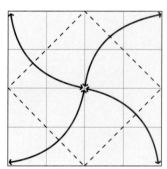

5 Use the installed mountain and valley creases to put the center of each edge and the four corners of the square to the center of the paper.

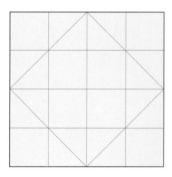

6 Paper in progress to center.

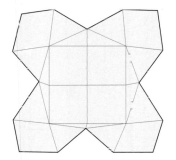

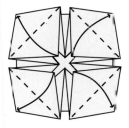

7 Valley-fold the four center corners to touch the four outer corners.

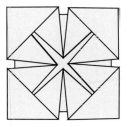

8 Finished flower unit.

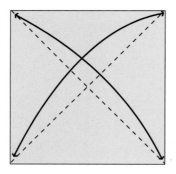 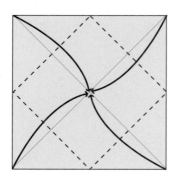 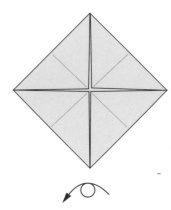

1 To begin the leaf unit, valley-fold and unfold the paper, corner-to-corner, both possible ways. This marks the center of the paper.

2 Valley-fold each of the four corners to the center of the paper.

3 Turn paper over.

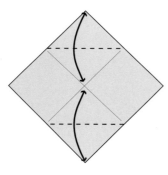

4 Valley-fold two opposite corners very close, but not precisely, to the center. Unfold these two points out again.

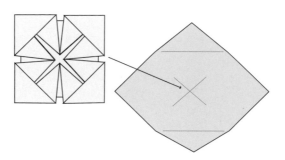

5 Place the flower unit in the center of the leaf unit.

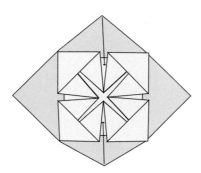

6 Tuck the two folded tab corners into the corner-shaped pockets of the flower unit.

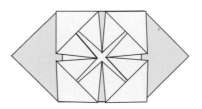

7 Assembled paper-fastening flower.

FASTENER

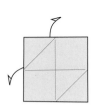

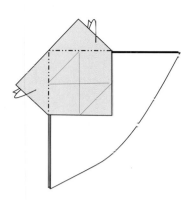

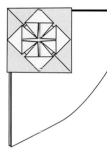

1 To fasten a few sheets of paper, take the paper-fastening flower apart and open two adjacent corners of the leaf paper. Be sure that this is done from a tab corner side.

2 Wrap these two opened corners around one corner of the papers to be fastened.

3 Place flower unit in center of leaf unit and retuck the two opposite tab corners of the leaf unit into the pockets flower unit.

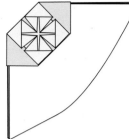

4 Fastened paper.

ENVELOPE

1 To make an envelope for a card use a square of suitable paper cut large enough to accommodate the size of your card as shown. Center the card diagonally and neatly fold two opposite corners of the envelope paper over to cover. The corners should overlap.

2 Fold remaining two corners over to cover. You will have overlapping corners again. Follow the imaginary, horizontal center line of the envelope to valley-fold these two corners out in such a way that they neatly form a square shape in the center of the envelope.

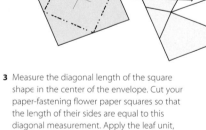

3 Measure the diagonal length of the square shape in the center of the envelope. Cut your paper-fastening flower paper squares so that the length of their sides are equal to this diagonal measurement. Apply the leaf unit, folding its four corners around the back of the center square form of the envelope.

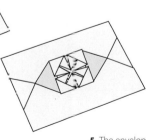

4 Center the flower unit and fold in the tab corners to lock.

5 The envelope is attractively and firmly sealed.

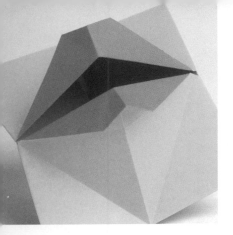

Talking Lips

Designed by Soon Young Lee
Diagrammed by Michael LaFosse

This delightful origami toy will surely become a favorite. Use it as a party favor or a surprise enclosure in a letter or card. For best effect use a paper that is colored differently on each side. Origami paper like this is commonly available; gift-wrap paper is often white on the back side. Use 6" (15 cm) squares for best results.

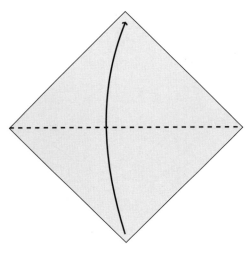

1 Begin with the colored side up. This is the color that the lips will be. Valley-fold bottom corner to top.

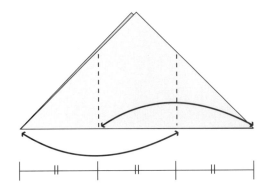

2 Valley-fold the bottom edge into even thirds, keeping the folded edges neatly aligned. Unfold. You will find it helpful later on if you take the time now to fold these same creases around the back (mountain-fold them) so that they are very flexible.

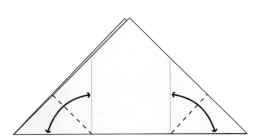

3 Valley-fold and unfold to crease lines.

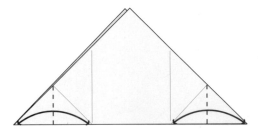

4 Valley-fold and unfold to points on the bottom folded edge.

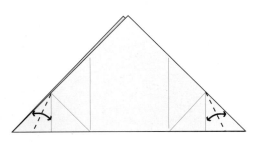

5 Valley-fold and unfold cut edges of the smaller triangle areas to the indicated crease lines.

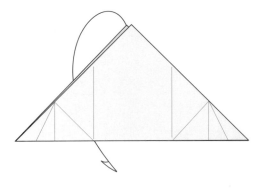

6 Open paper completely, wrong side up (not the lips color).

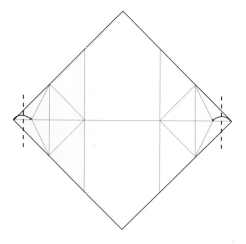

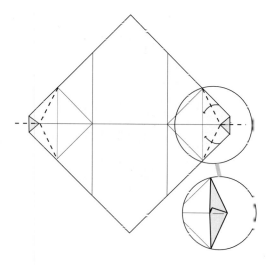

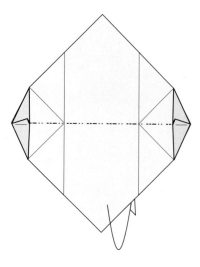

7 Valley-fold indicated corners to the first intersection of creases at each end of the diagonal crease line.

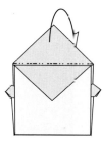

8 Use existing creases to valley-fold the indicated raw edges inward, lip color over non-lip color (see detail for final shape).

9 Use existing crease to mountain-fold paper in half.

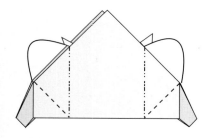

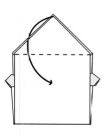

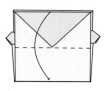

10 Use existing crease to push red paper lips inside. The lip papers will be in between the white, house-shaped paper layers.

11 The paper will look like this. Valley-fold the top, front corner down.

12 Mountain-fold the top colored corner down on the back.

13 Valley-fold the top folded edge to the bottom folded edge.

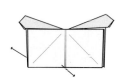

14 Mountain-fold the top folded edge to the back in the same manner.

15 Valley-fold the two white triangles down. Repeat behind. (In this flat form the lips can be included in a card or envelope.)

16 Pull on two opposite corners, one from each side, to open the lips

17 Finished lips.

18 Push and pull on the corners to make the lips talk.

Bucky Ball

Designed by Tom Hull

Diagrammed by Michael LaFosse

This ingenious folded-paper puzzle unit is easy to make and very versatile. You can fold many in a short time. Origami paper works very well, but a good choice of paper to use would be offset paper, which comes in many colors. Small squares, about 3" to 5" (7.62 cm to 12.70 cm) work best.

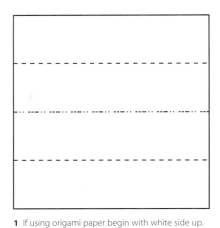

1 If using origami paper begin with white side up.

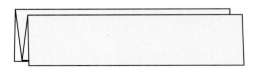

2 Mountain-fold and valley-fold the indicated creases to make a simple fan shape. Be sure the color ends up on the outside of the form.

3 Valley-fold the left-side, short, raw edge to the bottom long, raw edge.

4 Valley-fold the top long, folded edge to align with the folded edge of the triangle you formed in the previous step.

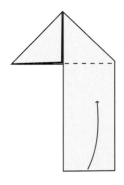

5 Valley-fold the long strip up.

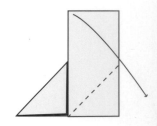

6 Valley-fold strip to the right, aligning all edges to the bottom.

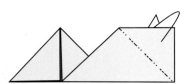

7 Mountain-fold the right-side corner to the back.

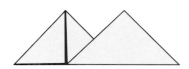

8 Finished unit.

You can construct all kinds of structures using this simple origami unit. Try forming a simple ball shape using thity pentagon-hexagon zigzag units. This will make a dodecahedron, which is the smallest closed form that you can make from this system. It is composed entirely of pentagon frames.

The buckminsterfullerene or Bucky Ball requires a minimum of ninety units. To make one you will build a structure with exactly twelve pentagon frame units, equally spaced apart as on the surface of a soccer ball, and separated by hexagon frames. You can make larger Bucky Balls by adding more hexagonal frames. One thing must stay constant: only twelve pentagon frames, equally spaced apart.

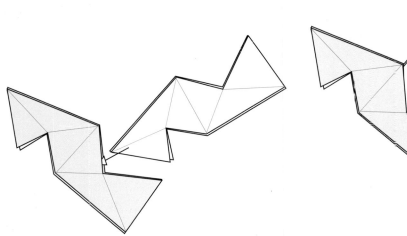

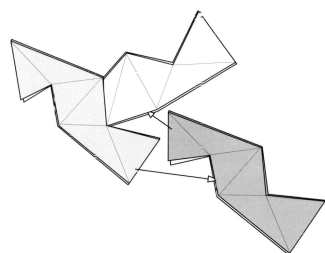

9 Assemble two units by inserting the narrow end of one between the open layers on the side of another. Carefully compare your work with the diagrams.

10 Add a third piece to make completed node. Notice how the narrow, free end of the two-piece assembly is inserted into the side of the newly added unit.

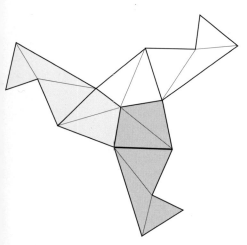

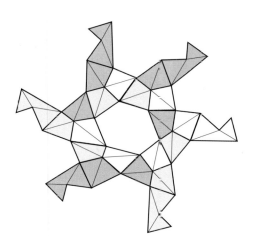

11 Finished three-piece node.

12 Here are six three-piece nodes assembled together. Notice how they form a hexagonal hole in the center of the assembly. Five nodes form a pentagonal hole. The holes effectively represent these polyhedra in frame form where only the edges are visible.

Flying Fox Airplane

Designed and diagrammed by Michael LaFosse

You may find this paper airplane design challenging at first, but once you master it you will see that it is very interesting and enjoyable to fold. The design, which incorporates all kinds of origami techniques, has great style, and is a fantastic flyer, too. Use a piece of paper that has a different color on each side to produce an attractive two-tone look. Look for origami duo papers for this effect. Otherwise, any thin, crisp paper will work very well. Cut your paper neatly square and install sharp creases for the best flight performance. Paper sizes of between 6" and 8" (15 cm and 20.32 cm) work best.

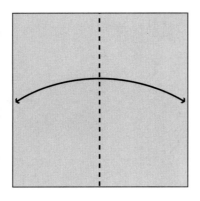

1 If using duo paper, begin with the color that you want to show on the leading edges of the wings and on the cockpit facing up. Valley-fold in half, edge to edge.

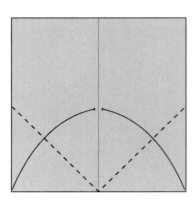

2 Valley-fold the two bottom corners to the center line.

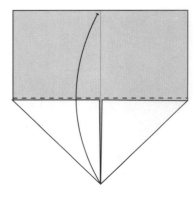

3 Valley-fold the bottom corner to the middle of the top edge.

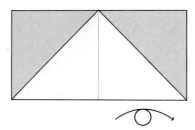

4 Turn model over, keeping the folded edge at the bottom of the paper.

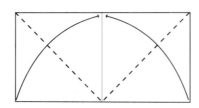

5 Valley-fold the two bottom corners to the top.

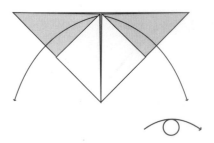

6 Unfold these two corners and turn the paper over. Again, keep the folded edge at the bottom.

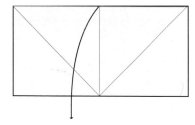

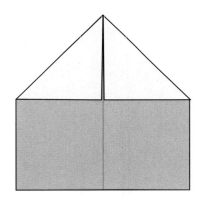

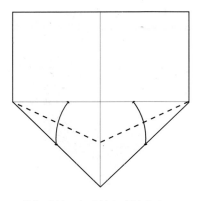

7 Unfold top, raw edge down.

8 Turn model over, top to bottom.

9 Valley-fold and unfold the folded edges to the horizontal centerline.

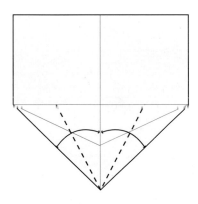

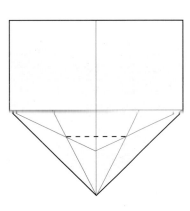

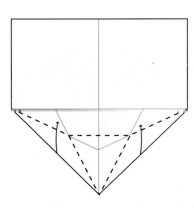

10 Valley-fold and unfold the folded edges to the vertical centerline.

11 Valley-fold a short crease between the intersections of the crossing crease lines.

12 Using the creases that are already in your paper, and indicated by dashed lines, form a standing half-pyramid shape in the nose-end of the paper.

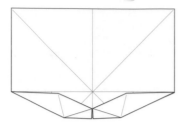

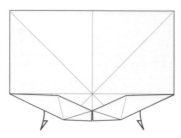

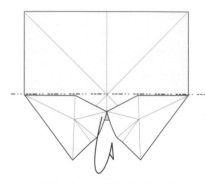

13 Using the creases that are already in your paper, and indicated by dashed lines, form a standing half-pyramid shape in the nose-end of the paper.

14 Bring out the loose corners of paper from underneath.

15 Position everything that lies below the horizontal centerline around the back of the paper, keeping its basic shape intact.

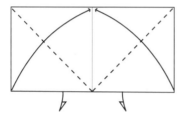

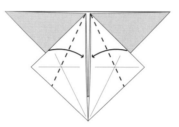

16 Valley-fold the two bottom corners to the top. The paper from the back will follow along and you should then be able to use all of the existing creases in this form to flatten the entire model out. Look ahead to the next diagram.

17 Valley-fold the two top, raw edges of the center shape to the centerline edges.

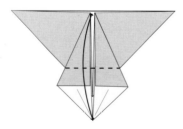

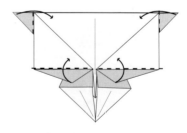

18 Pay close attention here to the two sets of arrows and the instruction to mountain-fold the smaller upper-layer of paper. This is technically referred to as a squash-fold. Look ahead to the next diagram to see where the separate layers must go. Valley-fold and unfold the bottom corner to the top.

19 Valley-fold each of the four indicated triangular areas of paper.

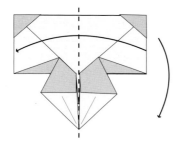 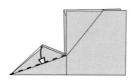

20 Valley-fold in half, wing-to-wing, and rotate the model to the position in the next diagram.

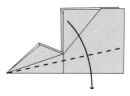

21 Valley-fold both of the indicated layers of paper into the pocket-like area of the nose. This effectively locks the nose of the plane closed: no tape or glue required.

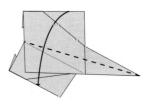

22 Fold the wing down, as flat as it can go.

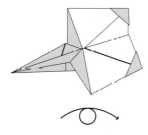

23 Notice that the wing angle is set by two limiting points: the nose point and the nose lock. The nose lock is at the back of the cockpit. Turn the model over.

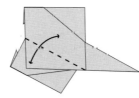

24 Prepare the back of the paper, to later form the vertical tail, by valley-folding and unfolding. The limits for this fold are between the V-shaped notch at the back of the two wings and the back bottom edge of the cockpit paper.

25 Valley-fold the other wing down to match the first.

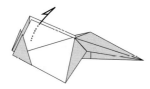

26 Pull the tail paper up and between the inside edges of the wing papers. The crease you installed in step 24 will guide you.

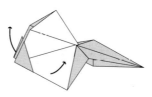

27 Open the wings level, on either side of the fuselage.

28 Stand the triangle-shaped stabilizers straight up on the back outside edges of the wings. The finished Flying Fox.

Preflight, check for symmetry of form and sharp creases. Launch like throwing a dart. Great indoors or out.

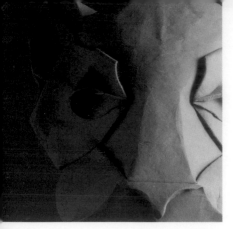

George L. Mountainlion

Designed and diagrammed by Michael LaFosse

This advanced project is best accomplished by wet-folding. The paper must first be dampened with a very light spray of water on each side before the actual folding begins. After spraying, the water droplets should be smoothed over the paper's surface for even wetting; a damp hand towel or a wide, soft-bristle brush is useful here. Heavier papers can be employed with this technique, so choose colored art papers, such as those used for charcoal and pastel drawing. Cut your paper to 18" (45.72 cm) square.

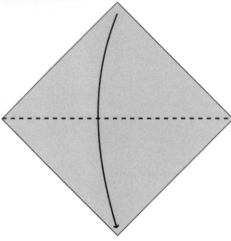

1 Valley-fold diagonally in half.

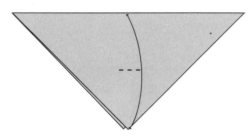

2 Pinch a mark in the paper halfway between the middle of the top edge and the bottom corner.

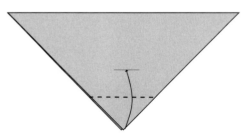

3 Valley-fold the top-layer corner to the middle of this pinch mark.

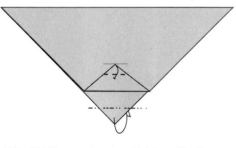

4 Valley-fold this corner about one third down; this will become the nose. Mountain-fold the bottom chin corner behind.

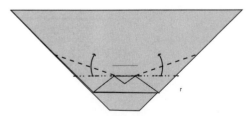

5 Mountain-fold and valley-fold in the cheek area up to 3-D the muzzle. Notice that each set of muzzle-forming creases originate at the outside corners of the nose.

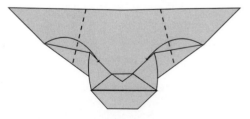

6 Valley-fold the wide corners, indicated, to touch the folded edges of the muzzle folds.

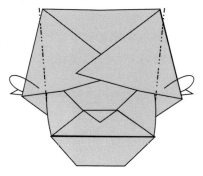

7 Mountain-fold around the back. Leave squares corners on the ears.

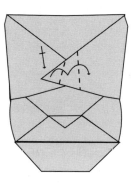

8 Form the eye papers by valley-folding over and over the pointed ends of the paper. Repeat for the other eye.

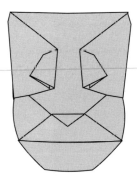

9 Mask will look like this. You can improvise all kinds of masks from this basic form. Turn model over.

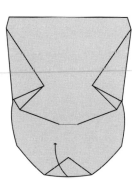

10 Lift chin paper up and out of the way.

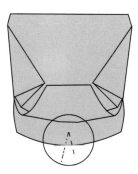

11 This is a crimp-fold (see details).

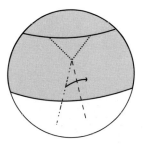

12 Mountain-fold and valley-fold to form a dart in the paper. Notice the X-ray view of the nose. The dart should start at the bottom point of the nose. Look on the other side of the paper as you work with it.

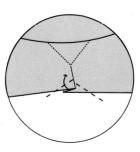

13 Lock the crimp in place and further form the upper lip by valley-folding the bottom third of the dart up. As you do this, let each layer go in opposite directions and then flatten.

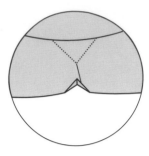

14 Lock the crimp in place and further form the upper lip by valley-folding the bottom third of the dart up. As you do this, let each layer go in opposite directions and then flatten.

15 Lower the chin paper back in place.

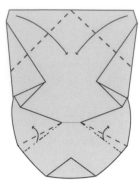

16 Crimp the inside of the lower jaw paper to allow it to better fit in the 3-D shape of the upper lip area just formed. Valley-fold the ears together to the center.

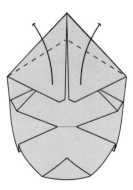

17 Valley-fold the ears out at a new angle.

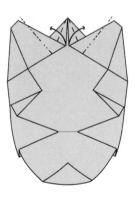

18 Mountain-fold and valley-fold the paper layers at the top of the head to further shape the ears.

19 The back of the mask should look like this. Turn model over.

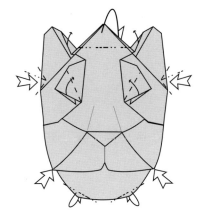

20 Mountain-fold the point of paper at the top of the head to the back. Shape the eyes, ears, cheeks, and chin with soft, rounded folds.

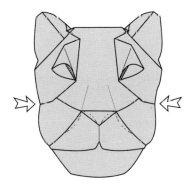

21 Narrow the middle of the face and install gently curved mountain creases for the nostrils and upper muzzle.

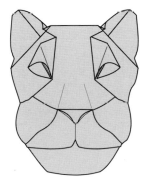

22 The finished mask.

Resources and Artist Directory

Following is a list of the artists, along with their projects, featured in this book. Where available, a published source is included for each model"s diagram so that you may learn to fold many of these wonderful designs.

Jeff Beynon
Hartham House
Hartham Park
Corsham
Wiltshire SN 13 OQB
UK
Contact through the British Origami Society
(see organizations)
Spring into Action: *Origami In Action* by Robert Lang, published by St. Martin's Press (ISBN 0-312-15618-9)

David Brill
UK
E-mail: davebrill@worthhall.demon.co.uk
Contact through the British Origami Society
(see organizations)
St. George and the Dragon: *Brilliant Origami by David Brill*, published by Japan Publications
(ISBN 0-87040-896-8)

Sy Chen
China/USA
http://users.erols.com/sychen1/pprfld.html
Contact through OrigamiUSA (see organizations)
Chinese Teapot and Cups

Edwin Corrie
Switzerland
E-mail: ecorrie@vtx.ch
Rhinoceros: *The New Origami* by Steve Megumi
Biddle, published by St. Martin's Press
(ISBN 0-312-08037-9)

Vincent Floderer
La Boissellerie - 19130 SAINT-AULAIRE
France
Mushrooms

Tomoko Fuse
Japan
Contact through Origami House (see organizations)
Jumping Frog: *UGOKU ORIGAMI* (*Moving Origami*)
by Tomoko Fuse, (ISBN 4-416-39210-9)
Triangle Boxes: *Origami Boxes* by Tomoko Fuse, published by Japan Publications (ISBN 0-87040-821-6)
Spires: *Origami Spirals*, by Tomoko Fuse, published by Chikuma Shobo (ISBN 4-480-87262-0)
Hannya Mask & Chidou Mask: *The Mask* by Tomoko Fuse, published by Origami House

Alfredo Giunta
Italy
Contact through Centro Diffusione Origami
(see organizations)
Fly : *Origami gli Insetti* by Alfredo Giunta, published by Il Castello Collane

Gay Merrill Gross
USA
E-mail: gay@origami-usa.org
Contact through OrigamiUSA (see organizations)
Paper Fastening Flower and Envelope: page 122 of this book.

Taichiro Hasegawa
Japan
Whirling Flower Tops

Tom Hull
USA
E-mail: thull@merrimack.edu
http://web.merrimack.edu/~thull/OrigamiMath.html
Five-Intersecting Tetrahedra:
http://web.merrimack.edu/~thull/fit.html
Bucky Ball: page 128 of this book and on
Tom's web site.

Paul Jackson
21 Hardwicke Road
London
N13 4SL
England
Abstract

Eric Joisel
22 Rue Louis Delamarre
Enghien-les-Bains
95880
France
Pangolin
America's Paper Cup®
Head of a Woman
Three Masks

Satoshi Kamiya
Contact through Japan Origami Academic Society
(see organizations).
Japan
Divine Dragon

Fumiaki Kawahata
Japan
Contact through Japan Origami Academic Society
(see organizations)
Stegosaurus: *Origami Fantasy* by Fumiaki Kawahata, published by Origami House (see organizations)

Kenneth M. Kawamura
USA
E-mail: kenny1414@aol.com
Contact through the Origamido Studio
(see organizations)
Butterfly Ball: *The Art of Origami* by Gay Merrill Gross, published by Michael Friedman Publishing Group, Inc.
(ISBN 0-7924-5841-9)

Miyuki Kawamura
Japan
Contact through Japan Origami Academic Society
(see organizations).
Cosmosphere

Toshikazu Kawasaki
Japan
Contact through Japan Origami Academic Society
(see organizations).
Rose & Leaf: Roses, Origami & Mathematics by
Toshikazu Kawasaki.
Field of Roses
Rock Crystal

Hideo Komatsu
Japan
Contact through Japan Origami Academic Society
(see organizations).
Tiger: *Tanteidan newsletter*,
Japan Origami Academic Society

Michael LaFosse
Origamido Studio
63 Wingate Street
Haverhill, MA 01832
USA
E-mail: michael@origamido.com
http:// www.origamido.com
Arizona Hummingbirds
Pinwheels and Sailboats
Big Brown Bat
Desert Scorpion and Praying Mantis.
Flying Fox: page 130 of this book.
Happy Good-Luck Bats - Videotape instruction:
"Happy, Good-luck Bats & Horseshoe Crab" by Michael
LaFosse, produced by Alexander Blace & Co. /
Origamido Studio (see organizations)
Aerogami (TM) Videotape instruction available:
"Planes for Brains" and *"AEROGAMI (TM)"* by Michael
LaFosse, produced by Alexander Blace & Co. /
Origamido Studio
George L. Mountainlion: page 134 of this book

Robert J. Lang
7580 Olive Drive
Pleasanton, CA 94588
USA
E-mail: rjlang@home.com
Allosaurus Skeleton
Black Forest Clock

Soon Young Lee
South Korea
Contact through Korea Jongie Jupgi Association
Institute of Paper Culture (see organizations)
Talking Lips: page 126 of this book

Luda Lezhneva
Russia
Contact through:
St. Petersburg Origami Center
c/o Sergei Afonkin
P.O. Box 377
St. Petersburg
193318 Russia
Matrioshka Dolls: *Russian Origami* by Sergei Afonkin
and Tom Hull, published by St. Martin's Griffin
(ISBN 0-312-16993-0)

John Montroll
Contact through Origamido Studio (see organizations)
Three-Headed Dragon: *Mythological Creatures and the Chinese Zodiac in Origami*, by John Montroll, published by Anroll Publishing Co. (ISBN 1-877656-11-9) and by Dover (ISBN 0-486-28971-0)
Chessboard and Pieces: *Origami Inside Out* by
John Montroll, published by Dover Publications
(ISBN 0-486-27674-0)

J.C. Nolan
USA
Contact through the Origamido Studio
(see organizations)
Clown Fish and Sea Anemone: *Creating Origami* by
J.C. Nolan, published by Alexander Blace & Co.,
Inc./Origamido Studio (ISBN 1-889856-02-9)

Francis Ow
Singapore
http://sunflower.singnet.com.sg/~owrigami/
Winged Hearts: *Origami Hearts* by Francis Ow, published by Japan Publications (ISBN 0-87040-957-3)

Chris Palmer
1227 Lorene Drive
Suite 12
Pasadena, MD 21122
USA
E-mail: ckpalmer@toad.net
http://www.cea.edu/sarah/chris
Pentagon Box with Pentagonal Star Flower Tower
Flower Tower Invitation
For study of Chris Palmer's techniques see *"The folding
techniques of Chris Palmer -
HIRA-ORI: Origami Boxes, Flowers and Tessellation,"* by
Chris K. Palmer, produced by Alexander Blace & Co. /
Origamido Studio (see organizations)

David Petty
UK
Contact through the British Origami Society
(see organizations)
Wreaths and Rings: *Origami Wreaths and Rings*
by David Petty, published by Zenagraf,
(ISBN 0-9627254-1-2)

Ethan Plaut
1335 Elmwood
Evanston, IL 60201
USA
E-mail: erp978@lulu.acns.nwu.edu
Geometric Composition
Landscape
Untitled Mask Composition
"Architectural Origami Design, Building on the
Triangle: The Many Facets of Ethan R. Plaut" (video)

Daniel Robinson
3310 W Coulter Street
Philadelphia, PA 19129
USA
Samurai Helmet Beetle
For a good origami insect collection try: *Origami
Insects and Their Kin* by Robert Lang,
published by Dover 1995 (ISBN: 0-486-28602-9)

Jeremy Shafer
USA
Contact through the Bay Area Rapid Folders (BARF)
(see organizations)
Flasher Hat and Labyrinth Walker: *"Bay Area Rapid
Folders Newsletter,"* Summer '98 issue, by Jeremy
Shafer, published by BARF

Gérard Ty Sovan
35, rue de Vigneronde - 95100 Argenteuil
Cambodia/France
Tel: (33) 01 34 11 39 21 Fax: (33) 01 39 82 53 28
Sailing Yacht

Hojyo Takashi
Japan
Contact through Japan Origami Academic Society
(see organizations).
Maitreya: *"Origami Tanteidan 4th Convention"*
publication, published by Origami Tanteidan
(now Japan Origami Academic Society)

Herman Van Goubergen
HofVan Tichelen 38
Antwerp
Belgium
E-mail: hvgouber@roam.agfa.be
Skull: *Annual Collection '99*, page 269,
published by OrigamiUSA.

Valerie Vann
USA
http://users.aol.com/valerivann/index.html
Contact through Origamido Studio (see organizations)
Magic Rose Cube: Instructions available on VHS "The
Origami of Valerie Vann, featuring the Magic Rose
Cube" through Origamido Studio

Joseph Wu
609 West 24th Avenue
Vancouver, BC, V5Z 2B7
Canada
Tel: 604-327-9891
Email: josephwu@ultranet.ca
http://www.origami.vancouver.bc.ca
Elephant
Rabbit

Makoto Yamaguchi
Gallery Origami House
1-33-8-216 Hakusan Bunkyou
Tokyo 112-0001
Japan
E-mail: origamih@remus.dti.ne.jp
http://www.remus.dti.ne.jp/~origamih
Ohinasama

Issei Yoshino
For information about Issei Yoshino and the
"Yoshino Fund" contact Japan Origami Academic
Society (see organizations).
Tyrannosaurus Rex Skeleton: *Origami T-Rex Skeleton*
by Issei Yoshino, published by Origami House
(see organizations listing)
Horse and Wild Boar: *Issei Super Complex Origami* by
Issei Yoshino, published by Origami House

Akira Yoshizawa
International Origami Center
PO Box 3
Ogikubo, Tokyo
Japan
Bison
Tops
Abstract
Buddha Mask
Shakyamuni
Further information can be found in: *Origami full of life
(Inochi Yutaka na Origami)* (Japanese text) by Akira
Yoshizawa, published by Sojusha (ISBN 4-916096-31-2)

Organizations

There are numerous organizations around the world devoted to paperfolding and advancing the art of origami. While the information listed below is current and accurate as this book goes to press, new organizations are being formed, while a few might disband. Changes are bound to occur. One of the best ways to keep current is to visit Joseph Wu's Origami page at www.origami.vancouver.bc.ca, or do a www search on the words Origami and Wu.

Argentina
Origamistas Argentinos
c/o Maria Susana Tanaka de Arashiro
Gorostiaga 1588
1426 Buenos Aires
Argentina

Australia
Clare Chamberlain
73 Harold Street
Mount Lawley
Western Australia 6050

Belgium
International Origami Center Belgium
I.O.C.B V2W,
Fr.v.d.Berghelaan 171
2630 Aartselaar
Belgium

Belgisch Nederlandse Origami Societeit
Postbus 49
B-2440 Geel
Belgium

Bolivia
Asociacion de Origami Boliviano-Japones
Casilla 3680
La Paz
Bolivia

Brazil
Centro Brasileiro de Difusao de Origami
c/o Carlos Eduardo Quillin
R. Honorio Libero 154
01445 Sao Paulo SP
Brazil

Canada
The Japanese Paper Place
887 Queen Street West
Toronto, M6J 1G5
Ontario
Canada

Quebec Origami
http://pages.infinit.net/crete/origami/

Columbia
Calle 146 A no 9545
Bogota
Colombia

Jose Tomas Buitrago Molina
Calle 57 26-45 apto 105
Palmira Valle
Columbia SA

Costa Rica
Asociacion Costaricense de Origami
Apartado 167
1001 San Jose
Costa Rica

Denmark
Dansk Origami Center
Ewaldsgade 4
KLD
2200 Kobenhavn-N
Denmark

France
Mouvement Francais des Plieurs de Papier
56 Rue Coriolis
75012 Paris
France

Germany
Origami Deutschland
Postfach 1630
8050 Freising
Germany

Great Britain
British Origami Society c/o Penny Groom
2A The Chestnuts
Countesthorpe
Leicester LE8 3TL
Great Britain
http://www.rpmrecords.co.uk/bos/

Hong Kong
The Chinese (HK) Origami Society
David Chan
Flat A 9/F
524 Nathan Rd.
Kowloon
Hong Kong
http://www.ap.net.hk/~cos

Hungary
Hungarigami
Kecskemet
pf.60
H-6000 Hungary

India
Origami Society of Calcutta
5/9/1 Khanpur Road
Calcutta 700047
India

Alapani
76 M.C.Ghosh Lane
Howrh-711 101
West Bengal
India

Israel
Israel Origami Society
c/o Rosaly Yevnin
Mevo HaAsara 1/22
97876 Jerusalem
Israel

Italy
CDO - Centro Diffusione Origami
Casella Postale 42
21040 Caronno Varesino (VA)
Italy
Tel. +39-331-775875
Email: cdo@essenet.it
http://www.essenet.it/CDO/

Origami
c/o Paolo Meschi
Via de Tofori 67
55010 Tofori
Lucca
Italy

Japan
Gallery Origami House
Makoto Yamaguchi
1-33-8-216 Hakusan Bunkyou
Tokyo 112-0001
Japan
Web site: www.remus.dti.ne.jp/~origamih
E-mail: origamih@remus.dti.ne.jp

Japan Origami Academic Society (Origami Tanteidan)
c/o Gallery Origami House
#216, 1-33-8, Hakusan
Bunkyo-ku, Tokyo
113-0001, JAPAN
Fax: 81/3/5684-6080
E-mail: webman@origami.gr.jp
http://origami.gr.jp/index.html

International Origami Centre
P.O. Box 3
Ogikubo
Tokyo 167
Japan

Nippon Origami Association
2-064 Domir Gobancho
12-Gobancho
Chiyoda-ku
Tokyo 102
Japan

Korea
Korea Jongie Jupgi Association Institute
of Paper Culture
5F Sukama Bldg 189
Dongsoong-Dong
Jongno-ku
Seoul, Korea

KJJA D.H.Chung
3/4 F Sukma Building
1089 Dongsoong Dong
Jongno-Ku
Seoul 110-510
Korea

Mexico
Federation Internacional de Origami de Mexico A.C.
Providencia 520
Col del Valla
Mexico, D.F.C.P.03100

Netherlands
Origami Societeit Nederland
Mossinkserf 33
7451 XD Holten
The Netherlands

De Vuyst Origami
Postbus 427
5460 AK Veghel
The Netherlands

New Zealand
New Zealand Origami Society
79 Dunbar Road
Christchurch 3
New Zealand

Peru
Centro Latino de Origami
Caracas 2655
Dpto. 13-Jesus Maria
Lima 11
Peru

Poland
Polskie Centrum Origami
Szkoza Podstanowa nr 20
os. Rzeczypospolite 44
Poznan 775631
Poland

Russia
The Union of Soviet Societies for Friendship &
Cultural Relations
Noskva
K - 9 Prospekt
Kalinina 14
Russia

St. Petersburg Origami Center
193318 Russia
St. Petersburg
P.O. Box 377
cher. Sergei Afonkin

Club Kenrokuen
Gerscheritcha 2-19
664000 Irkutsk
Russia

Singapore
c/o Francis M.Y. Ow
Blk 127
Tampines Street 11
#02-404
Singapore 1852

Spain
Asociación Española de Papiroflexia
Julian Gonzalez Garcia Gutierrez
Maria Guilhou 2-3 C
28016 Madrid
Spain

Grupo Zaragozano de Papiroflexia
P.O. Box 11.073
50080 Zaragoza
Spain

Tanzania
c/o A.R.Mgeni
P.O. Box 9423
Dar Es Salaam
Tanzania

U.S.A
Bay Area Rapid Folders (BARF)
Jeremy Shafer
1744 Virginia St.
Berkeley, CA 94703 USA
E-mail: jugami@krmusic.com
http://www.krmusic.com/barf.htm

OrigamiUSA
15 West 77th Street
New York, NY 10024-5192
(212) 769-5635
http: www.origami-usa.org

Venezuela
Asociacion de Origami Venezolana
Av.Circunvalacion No 188
Las Mariase
El Hatillo - EDO
Miranda
Venezuela

Glossary

Abaca: Manila Hemp, *Musa textilis* "Banana." The fibers from the lining of the bark of this plant is used to make strong papers.

Back-coating: The process of pasting together two or more sheets of folding materials (paper, foil, fabric).

Color-change: When folding paper with two different color sides, it is sometimes possible to change the color of an origami structure by reversing its display surface.

Compound origami: Constructions of origami; usually with each piece folded differently, as in the folding of an animal from two or more pieces of paper. Paste is usually employed in compound models.

Duo-paper: Folding paper that is a different color on each side. Though standard origami paper is white on one side and colored on the other, the applied term, "duo," is mostly reserved for papers with no white side.

Inside-Out origami: A technique showing both sides of two-colored paper in the finished model. The talking lips and the chessboard are a good examples.

Kozo: Mulberry (*Broussonetia kajinoki*) an important plant used in the making of washi.

Momigami: Hand-crumpled, Japanese washi.

Model: An origami project. Mostly refers to the finished origami but is often applied to the object during folding as well.

Modular origami: Origami constructions of two or more folded units, or "modules." Assembly does not require any adhesives. Most modulars are constructed of sets of identically folded units and are rather like puzzles in their way of assembly.

Unit origami: see Modular origami.

Washi: The handmade paper of Japan.

Wet fold: A technique of folding paper while moist, allowing the sizing to soften, lubricating the paper fibers to bend and not break. Moistening the area to be creased overcomes hydrogen bonding, and prevents fiber breaking in the process.

Index of Artists

Photo Credits

All photos by Kevin Thomas, except for the following:

Richard Alexander: 6-7, 9 (bottom)
Aaron Caplan: 35, 36-37, 81
Bob Hart: 86, 87, 118
Mike Howard: 56 (top)
Miyuki Kawamura: 88
Michael Lafferty: 17, 101
Larime Photographic: 66-67
Nakajima: 112
Yagi Shinji: 5 (bottom), 76, 105, 107
Hojyo Takahashi: 108
Michiko Yajima: 40, 41
Akira Yoshizawa: cover, 9, 38, 59, 85, 94, 111

ACKNOWLEDGMENTS

It has been my privilege to assemble the works of many of the world's finest origami artists for this book. The great variety of style, technique, and philosophy among the artists makes this an especially interesting and valuable collection. There are so many talented origami artists, too many to fit into one volume! I apologize to those many other deserving origami artists who are not represented here. I hope that this book will inspire more such publications and add a rich new venue for the exhibition and appreciation of the art of origami, which is truly experiencing its golden age.

Coordinating the efforts of artists from a dozen different countries requires the enthusiastic efforts of many people. Fortunately for me, this group of contributors and facilitators was willing and able, and I am indebted to them all.

Origamidō is an important first in the field of books about origami. A photographic treatment and presentation of fine origami design was long overdue and I am indeed grateful to Rockport Publishers for their faith in, and support of, this book. Presentation sets the tone for interpretation and I am grateful for the talent and thoughtfulness that graphic designer Leeann Leftwich has contributed to the layout of this book. My deep appreciation and thanks go to the bright and talented staff at Rockport Publishers, most especially to Martha Wetherill, acquisitions editor; Cathy Kelley, art director; and Francine Hornberger, project manager. Their enthusiasm, guidance, and hard work helped shape the material into a marvelous and inspiring presentation. I thoroughly enjoyed working with them all.

Thanks to those who aided me in contacting and communicating with our many overseas contributors: Sergei Afonkin, Jonathan Baxter, Jan Polish, Paul Jackson, Robin Macey, David Brill, Sara Giarrusso, Joseph Wu, the Korea Jongie Jupgi Association Institute of Paper Culture, OrigamiUSA, and especially Hatori Koshiro, who acted as interpreter and patiently conveyed my many questions and requests for art of the Japanese contributors. Surely, this would not have been as "international" without their generous help. Special thanks to Gareth Morfill for folding the example of Tom Hull's *Five Intersecting Tetrahedra*, pictured on page 71.

Wherever possible, we asked the contributing artists to send their delicate and precious work to us to be photographed professionally by the exacting, yet good-humored, Kevin Thomas. His skill as a photographer and his appreciation for the art of origami are both apparent in his sumptuous photographs. I truly enjoyed working with him at these photo sessions.

Special thanks goes to my partner, Richard Alexander, cofounder of the Origamido Studio, and editor of many drafts of this book. Without his generosity and behind-the-scenes efforts, this book would not have been possible.

I am most especially indebted to Yoshizawa Akira sensei, Tokyo, Japan. He, his wife, and his sister-in-law have been most generous, and their hard work and dedication to the art of origami are legendary. It was the example of Mr. Yoshizawa's superb origami that opened my eyes to the creative and artistic possibilities of folded paper. I am deeply thankful for the time they have given me and my contemporaries through the many workshops, lectures, and exhibits that they have developed. Yoshizawa's extraordinary art has been an inspiration to countless people throughout the world, and will continue in this way for many generations to come.